PRACTICAL LAW

CHESTER S. WEINERMAN maintains an active general practice of law in Boston, Massachusetts. A graduate of the University of Massachusetts/Amherst and Case Western Reserve University School of Law, he is also a lecturer in law at The Cambridge Center for Adult Education and has given numerous other speeches before a wide range of audiences.

PRACTICAL LAW

A LAYPERSON'S HANDBOOK

CHESTER S. WEINERMAN

PRENTICE-HALL, INC., Englewood Cliffs, New Jersey 07632

Library of Congress Cataloging in Publication Data

Weinerman, Chester S
  Practical law.

  (A Spectrum Book)
  Includes index.
  1. Law—United States—Popular works.   I. Title.
  KF387.W39   340'.0973   77-26164
  ISBN 0-13-691113-7
  ISBN 0-13-691105-6 pbk.

A Spectrum Book

10 9 8 7 6 5 4 3 2

Printed in the United States of America

PRENTICE-HALL INTERNATIONAL, INC., *London*
PRENTICE-HALL OF AUSTRALIA PTY. LIMITED, *Sydney*
PRENTICE-HALL OF CANADA, LTD., *Toronto*
PRENTICE-HALL OF INDIA PRIVATE LIMITED, *New Delhi*
PRENTICE-HALL OF JAPAN, INC., *Tokyo*
PRENTICE-HALL OF SOUTHEAST ASIA PTE. LTD., *Singapore*
WHITEHALL BOOKS LIMITED, *Wellington, New Zealand*

**TO THE MEMORY OF MY FATHER
AND THE HONOR OF MY MOTHER**

Contents

Preface   **xiii**

Introduction   **1**

I

WRITTEN INSTRUMENTS

1

Contracts   5

Consideration / Understanding / Offer and Acceptance
Types of Revocation / Parole Evidence
Voidable and Unenforceable Contracts
Contracts That Aren't Really Contracts
Other Types of Contracts
Measure of Damages / Rules of Thumb

2

Landlord–Tenant Law   30

*Finding an Apartment   /   Tenants under a Lease
Tenancies without Leases   /   Eviction   /   Rent Withholding
Rent Control   /   Tips to Remember*

3

Buying and Selling a House   52

*Real Estate Listings   /   The Binder
The Purchase and Sale Agreement   /   Shopping for a Mortgage
Processing the Mortgage   /   The Closing   /   Tips to Remember*

4

Insurance   77

*Insurance Today   /   The Insurance Binder   /   Life Insurance
Health and Accident Policies   /   Fire Insurance
Automobile Insurance   /   Tips to Remember*

5

Wills and Trusts   97

*Requirements of a Will   /   Changing the Will
Execution of the Will   /   Contents and Omissions
Trusts in a Will   /   Intestacy   /   Should You Make a Will?*

II

OTHER LEGAL TOPICS

6

The Law of Torts 121

What Is a Tort? / Intentional Torts / Privileges
Negligence / Misrepresentation / Defamation
Nuisance / Interference with Contractual Relations
Liability for Torts

7

Your Consumer Rights 152

Void or Voidable Consumer Contracts / Automobiles
Household Goods / Advertising and Promotion Services
Credit / Regulated Industries / Conclusion

8

The Legal Rights of
Minorities 172

Lack of Upward Mobility / Rights Minorities Are Given
Laws Protecting Women / The Fourteenth Amendment
Other Minority Protections / Minority Rights in Reality Today

9

Criminal Law and the
Criminal Process 194

Criminals and Crimes / The Pre-trial Process
The Trial / Conclusion

10

Choosing a Lawyer

236

The General Practitioner or the Specialist
Advertising and Fees / Large Firm or Sole Practitioner
City Lawyer or Local Lawyer / Other Legal Help
Dissatisfaction with Your Lawyer
How Do You Know for Sure?

Index

249

Preface

The presentation of diverse areas of the law in a manner that will be easily understood by readers with equally diverse purposes is a formidable task. This is not the first book to attempt an explanation of laws that affect us as laypeople; unfortunately most of its predecessors seem to be burdened with the monotone of a frustrated law school text. Even worse, many have taken on the length and air of a heavy encyclopedia one would fear to disturb as it gathers dust.

This book does not pretend that what is written herein is simple. A great amount of legal theory and practical knowledge is set forth in a compact space. Only the chapter on criminal law, the longest section of the book, is both detailed and relatively unabridged. Inasmuch as the remainder of the book is devoted to civil law, and the complex procedures of criminal law are vastly misunderstood (even by lawyers), it would be a disservice to abbreviate this section. Only by a clear understanding of how the criminal system works can we as citizens intelligently deal with the dysfunction of our time.

One chapter of the book concentrates on minority rights, a subject that is not a clear-cut set of principles, as is contract law or home conveyancing. To consider the legal rights of minorities without a pervasive sociological overview is to grasp at relatively meaningless laws out of the framework within which laws are made, changed, and ignored.

The discussion of minority rights takes no new positions. Modern sociologists, psychologists, and criminologists are all schooled in the effects of the "haves" versus the "have-nots" and the need for the powerful to retain power. That minorities are allowed only those rights that the majority is willing to grant is as relevant conceptually as an inconsistent court decision or repealable statute or unbudgeted enforcement agency. All must be considered together.

To view minority rights only in terms of existing statutes and bureaucratic options is in fact irrelevant. The chapter accordingly takes some firm positions, with the hope of generating dissenting thought and class discussion that ultimately will prove more consonant with the goals of true education. The author expects disagreement, although he hopes that the opposition, in the great British tradition, will be loyal to the morals and hopes of genuine justice and the ideals promulgated in any genuinely democratic society.

I wish to extend my sincere appreciation to several people who have assisted in the toil of this treatise. First, Martin R. Rosenthal, Esq., of the Massachusetts Defenders Committee, gave unselfishly of his time and his knowledge of criminal law to help fashion a complete and practical approach to the chapter on criminal law. He has been a friend for fifteen years and a professional associate since we first became lawyers in the same class.

Louis Birenbaum of Suffolk Law School and Linda Giles, a graduate of the New England School of Law and former legal assistant for the Massachusetts Consumers' Council, lent their invaluable assistance toward the completion of the chapters on torts and consumer rights, respectively.

Sharon Lanciani and Phyllis Weinerman assisted in the typing of the drafts of these chapters, and their patience under pressure deserves admiration.

My gratitude is especially expressed to Sydney S. Rosen, Esq., and the Cambridge Center for Adult Education, both of whom gave me opportunities early in my career without which the realization of this book would have been an impossibility.

Finally, my thanks to Robert West, now of The Duxbury Press and Spade & Archer, for creating and initiating this project and placing trust in an unknown commodity; and to Michael Hunter and Prentice-Hall, Inc. for their gracious implementation of the idea.

Introduction

What exactly is meant when we speak of "the law"? The law within our legal system derives from two sources: One body of law is created by our various legislatures and codified into written laws known as *statutes*; the other body of law, known as *case law*, is propounded on a case-by-case basis by the appellate courts. No law is absolute; both bodies of law are subject to possible modification, repeal, or reversal. For this reason, no book on the law can profess to be a definitive work; it can at best be used as a guide through the often tangled webs of American jurisprudence. Similarly, as each state has its own legislatures and court system, fifty separate bodies of law have evolved. Although common principles unite them, no law book with a nationwide distribution can attempt to provide more than a broad synthesis of the most fundamental theories and widespread practices in the law.

This book is not meant to take the place of a lawyer. It is

designed to tell the lay reader or student how to recognize and avoid legal pitfalls and how to know when it's time to hire a lawyer. Anyone who attempts to draw his own will or to execute his own purchase and sales agreement has the proverbial fool for the client; in cases of self-representation, a penny saved today is often a thousand dollars spent later.

The overview herein presented is to guide you to understand law in a way that is meaningful in your day-to-day life. By studying its contents, you may be less likely to need a lawyer, because you will have become aware of things most people don't know how to look for. When you need a lawyer, you will be able to use his or her services more intelligently, thereby saving you time and money.

There is no substitute for professional advice, and there are few comforts as great as an ongoing relationship with a trusted attorney. Although not every attorney is worthy of that trust, most of them are. It is a profession more honest and diligent than the general public realizes, and the high fees sometimes charged are usually earned.

It is important, however, that each person have an elementary understanding of the laws and practices that operate upon us all in day-to-day life, when a lawyer is not always readily available. To that end, the information in this book should be required learning, as much as are algebra and history. Unlike these more traditional disciplines, what you are about to read will be applicable directly in repeated instances, perhaps as soon as tomorrow.

I

WRITTEN INSTRUMENTS

1

Contracts

The large print giveth and the small print taketh
away—Tom Waits

We enter into agreements every day of our lives. Those
agreements or promises which are legally enforceable are
called *contracts*.

A contract is not necessarily a formal document on crisp
parchment with seals and ribbons; it does not have to be in
writing or even be expressed in words. As long as an understanding is reached between parties having the legal capacity
to agree and some value is exchanged between them, then a
contract may be formed to which the parties may be held
liable or responsible.

It is vital to remember that when you enter into an
agreement you may at some later date either be bound by it
or attempt to bind someone else to it. Contracts cannot affect
the past; they are made for some present or future perfor-

mance. The difficulty of proving the existence and contents of the agreement is the substance of most common contractual controversies. Phrases like: "He promised he'd do it," "I thought we had an understanding," and "I trusted him," are the touching but useless soliloquies of victims left unable to *prove* the existence of an alleged agreement. This failure to grasp the requirements of the breached contract too often leaves people with enormous financial and emotional losses. Gaining a basic understanding of contract law will help you to avoid the aggravation experienced by laypeople unfamiliar with what *can* go wrong.

Not all promises are contracts. If I promise to clean your house every day, you cannot sue me for breach of contract if I suddenly stop cleaning it. However, if I promise to clean your house if you pay me one hundred dollars a week in advance, and you do pay me and I stop in the middle of the week, you may under a theory of contracts be entitled either to some additional cleaning or to a return of a portion of your money. The difference between these two examples partially is the existence of "consideration."

CONSIDERATION

In every contractual agreement it is a basic tenet that something of value must be exchanged; otherwise, there will not be an enforceable agreement. One must surrender *something* to receive *something*, be it a service or an act or the exchange of another promise or money. This exchange of value is known as *consideration*. The basis for much of the material in this chapter, this concept is easily remembered when one stops to think of the *lack of consideration* inherent in enforcing an arrangement that was to the sole benefit of one party. In consideration of fairness, the law operates to ensure that each party receives some value for the performance of his end of the agreement before it will declare that contractual agreement to be valid. Often, however, this benefit will for one party merely be the completion of a service or act he requests that may appear to offer him no direct benefit. His consideration is accomplished by his "getting his way."

It is for this reason that the promise of a gift is not legally enforceable. The person to whom the gift is promised is not giving up anything of value. All he has lost is the expectation of enrichment. Had the gift been predicated upon his prior performance, however, as we shall discuss in a moment, then it may no longer be considered simply a gift, and in such cases the donor of the so-called gift may be compelled to make good on the delivery of the "gift" that would be rightly forthcoming where the donee had given some consideration.

Consideration may be satisfied in several ways. If Ann promises Betty something, Ann becomes the *promisor* and Betty becomes the *promisee*. Ann has given up something. It is not a contract yet because the promisee has not on her part had to give up anything. But if Angus promises Beulah something and in exchange or in consideration thereof Beulah promises something to Angus, then both parties have given up something to get something, and the requirement for consideration will have been met. An exchange of promises is one way to arrive at a binding agreement.

In the case of a service or an act, the commencement of the performance of the act at the request of the promisor would satisfy consideration. To paraphrase an ancient homily, he who asks the piper to play must pay for the tune. Having performed as requested, the piper would have a legal cause of action if the promisor, knowing of his obligation to pay, tried stealthily to turn away.

Something must have been given up to which a party had a right in order to satisfy consideration. Neighbor Nancy cannot enforce a promise made to pay her a weekly ransom for not trespassing on Patrick's petunia bed, because she did not possess the right initially to trespass on Patrick's land. In fact, Nancy had a *pre-existing duty* not to commit trespass and thus was giving up nothing for her pay. The requirement of consideration would fail, and hence, she would be unsuccessful in litigation (in a lawsuit) were she to sue Patrick for his cessation of payments.

If, on the other hand, Nancy promised to build for him a ten-foot swimming pool provided that at the end of a year Patrick successfully maintained her petunia bed, Patrick's performance and subsequent demand for Nancy to install the pool would be enforceable. Patrick would argue under a contract theory that he had tenderly nurtured the garden all year with the incentive and purpose of swimming in his own pool. He gave up all that time and labor as his *consideration* or *value* and was now entitled to value for value: to wit, a swimming pool, as promised by Nancy.

Once in court, Nancy might counter-argue that no such agreement ever existed between them, that Patrick raised the petunias for his own ego, or that she never would have made such an expensive commitment for something as silly as a bed of flowers. She might prevail, much to Patrick's chagrin, because of Patrick's inability to *prove* the existence of the contractual arrangement.

Forbearance and Legal Detriment

Refraining from doing an act one would otherwise have the right to do will also generally suffice as consideration, a type legally referred to as *forbearance*. If Daddy promises Jennifer a trip to Marrakech if she completes college, Jennifer may legally be able to hold her father to that express contract. She had abstained from running off to New York or becoming a working person or a socialite and had instead remained in school as her father wished. She had given value and was entitled to the return value as promised. The same result would hold if her father had promised her that trip if she stopped smoking cigarettes. Her consideration would be her forbearance from an activity she would otherwise be performing and have the right to perform. She acted in each case to her *legal detriment*, and Daddy received the benefits he requested. In both cases, for the father to renege on the trip would be a breach of his contractual obligations in view of her performance or forbearance from performing. If Daddy had simply promised her a trip and then changed his mind, with no performance required on her part, then she would have no legal recourse because she had given up nothing.

UNDERSTANDING

Consideration is not the only requirement necessary for a valid contract. There must also be an *understanding* between the parties that they have mutually assented to something and what that something actually is. That understanding may not be taken for granted by either party, but must be expressed or in certain rarer cases implied by tacit actions. This understanding is most often manifested through an *offer* made by one party and an *acceptance* in response to that specific offer by another party.

Offer and Acceptance

An offer must be made (by the *offeror*) in clear and precise terms and must give to the other party (the *offeree*) the power to accept that offer. The offeree must believe that the offeror intended for him to either accept or reject the offer and thereby form a contract. When the intention of either party is in dispute, the courts will usually look to the words, circumstances, actions, and prior dealings between the parties to ascertain whether or not a contract was agreed to.

For example, if Barry tells Ray that he will sell him his sailboat as soon as he gets tired of it, to which Ray replies "Sure!", Ray cannot later bind Barry to that offer, because it was not in definite enough terms. A time was not specifically set for the sale. Neither was a price agreed upon. The conditions were far too uncertain to actually give Ray the ability to conclude a contract by accepting. Now suppose Barry's offer to Ray had included a definite time and price, but that at the appropriate time Ray's friend Henry tells Barry that *he* is accepting the offer because Ray isn't interested. In this case there would still be no contract, even though Barry's terms to Ray were totally acceptable to Henry. The reason is that Barry did not intend to give Henry the right to accept the offer and thereby conclude the contract. The offer was made to Ray, and only Ray had the power to accept.

This hypothetical situation is illustrative of numerous problems caused by people who erroneously think they are parties to binding contracts. If the agreement is not made in your presence or directly to you in writing and with you as a principal, it is wisest to assume that you are *not* going to be protected. Too often one associate will sign an agreement while his other associates are off doing other things. The other associates may want the protection or right of being a part of the agreement and may assume that his signature will bind them all. Unfortunately, depending on what the trust, partnership agreement or corporate by-laws may say, they may or may not be bound or protected. It may well turn out that only the signators to the contract are bound, and many people lose control over the management of their affairs and investments as a result. It is most unwise to trust someone who tells you "You'll have control, don't worry," if the agreement does not make you a party to it. This may also hold true for leases, which are a type of contract and which will be discussed in greater detail in the following chapter on landlord and tenant rights. It is always wise to insist on being a named party to an agreement and signing that agreement in instances where you want to be a party to that agreement.

Definiteness. The more definite the communication of the offer, the greater the chance that it will be held to be a valid offer that can be accepted. The spelling out of time, place, price, quantity, and merchandise contributes toward the presumption that the offeror has the intent to give the offeree the ability to accept the offer.

Advertisements and Mail Orders. Neither inquiries nor answers to inquiries nor advertisements are considered to constitute offers. They are generally considered to be a part of commercial dealings for the purpose of informing a segment of the public which goods or services potentially are available at certain terms upon which an offer may subsequently be made. Thus, if Bud wires Nick asking him how much beer he will sell at the lowest possible price and Nick wires in response that he will sell 500 cases at $4.00 per case and that the offer will stay open for one week, Nick's reply will probably not constitute an offer, if he does not specifically say he will sell the order to Bud. It is only a response to an inquiry.

In another widely used practice, certain businesses send out information telling a recipient that unless they receive a response within a certain number of days, they will assume he is agreeable to the terms of their offer. In actuality, such an arrangement is not an offer but an invitation to make an offer. Additionally, silence generally will *not* constitute an acceptance. In order to accept an offer, there must be a clear communication from the offeree (the person to whom the offer is made), either expressly or by implied conduct, that he wishes to accept the offer. Think of the millions of people today who would otherwise be bound to contracts by slick mail-order houses who might have the resources to inundate consumers with such "conditional offers" through the mails! How many rejections would fail to be returned because of the quantities of the circulars, the busy schedules of us all, the general confusion of what unknown and unsolicited business could be requiring us to do?

Other businesses will send to you goods in the mail and tell you that "two-fingered gnomes hand-crafted the enclosed ball point pens and the least you can do is send five dollars to defray the cost of the pens." Too often, people send in the requested amount of money, feeling either that they must help out the gnomes or that they aren't entitled to keep something for free that was sent to them.

You are under no contractual obligation to pay for the unsolicited goods, not having asked for them. The wisest thing to do is to send the goods back to the concern and demand to be taken off their mailing list. If the item will cost you money to return, then notify the company by mail that you are holding the merchandise for them to either fetch or until such time as they send you the proper amount of money necessary for return postage and handling. The mere receipt of something of value does not establish a contract.

Many record clubs and book clubs operate in this fashion. However, when you agree to join them, you usually agree *in advance* to accept their "selection of the month" unless you notify the club prior to their cut-off date for shipment. This is a condition of your membership to which you probably agreed at the time you offered to join their club on those terms. Be certain to read the terms of these club memberships with extreme care prior to ordering your six "free" records or your twelve "free" books, because your contract may prove to be more costly in the long run than had you shopped at wholesale prices for just the commodities you actually desired. Too often the result of joining these clubs is buying costly monthly selections you didn't want, only because you forgot to send in your rejection on time. If you *agree* that silence will constitute acceptance in a particular transaction, then you will be bound legally to that understanding.

Advertisements are generally considered not to constitute offers. This is true whether the advertisement is in a newspaper, a catalog, or a circular, or on television or radio. Rather, advertisements are considered to be solicitations for which you are invited to make an offer. The reason for this rule is quite sensible. A merchant should be permitted to make known what goods and services he has to sell without binding himself to a contract by making that information available to the public. If Funky Furniture offers a three-piece bedroom set for $97, you cannot walk in off the street and tell them you accept their contractual offer. They have given you information that enables you to come in as an offeror and offer them $97 for the set. Funky might have a hundred such sets in stock, but if 10,000 people are at the door at nine in the morning to purchase a set, then obviously everyone will not be satisfied. The other 9,900 cannot sue Funky for a breach of contract, because there was no contract. Funky was only making known to the public its available merchandise.

Note that this does not mean Funky could advertise a set of furniture for $97 and then not have the set in stock at all, or only have two sets in stock, or under a "bait and switch" tactic try to sell you a set at a greatly increased price once you came to the store. All of these tactics may be violations of state or Federal consumer laws and other relevant state statutes, and Funky might be liable to you on one of these grounds. But there would not be a breach of contract, because Funky's advertisement was not intended to give you the power to bind the firm contractually by accepting its offer. This will be discussed at greater length when we take up consumer laws.

There is one exception to the rule that advertisements do not constitute offers that can be accepted by the offeree. An advertisement that applies to or can be answered by only one person or a limited class of people may be accepted through performance of the offeree. For example, if a $50 reward is offered in the local newspaper for finding Fido, a lost Persian cat, and you find Fido, you are entitled to that $50 reward. Only one person in effect could accept that offer for a reward, and it is thus distinguishable from a department store ad for furniture, which is intended for the public at large and which is really not an offer but an invitation.

Prior Course of Dealing. The one major exception to the rule that silence does not constitute acceptance is where a prior course of dealing in an understood practice of the particular type of transaction will equal acceptance. The most common example is your automobile insurance. In most states, your car insurance will be renewed automatically unless you specifically notify the company that you do not wish to renew with them by the final day of the policy's effective date. Subscriptions to newspapers are also continued automatically unless you notify the distributor that you are cancelling, and it's a good idea to do this in writing. Otherwise the paper boy you told may forget to inform the distributor, denying you ever told him anything about cancellation, and you will have no proof otherwise. A carbon copy of your notice of cancellation is of far greater value than the plaintive cry of "But I *told* him."

Termination of Offer

Rejection. Now let us suppose that an offer has been made to you that after examination you find to be unacceptable. In order to best protect yourself, you should communicate that rejection to the offeror in a definite and positive manner. In fact, a rejection is not considered effective until it has been made known to the offeror, and it is best, though no longer required, to make that rejection in the same form that the offer was originally communicated. Thus, if the offer was made by telegram, it is safest to reject it by telegram, or at least by some provable writing. Oral rejections of written offers are unwise and often ineffective because, once again, they are difficult to substantiate beyond "your word against his."

Counter-offers. Outright rejection is not the only way to terminate an offer. If Doug offers Julie his Fiat for four hundred dollars, Julie may say, "That's too much money. I'll offer to pay you three hundred dollars." In effect, she has made Doug a *counter-offer* that operates both as a rejection of Doug's original offer and as a new offer on her part to which Doug then has the right to accept or reject. Julie has become the new offeror and Doug the offeree. If Doug in turn says, "No, but you can buy it for three hundred and fifty dollars," he has rejected her counter-offer and has become the offeror again. If Julie accepts, then a contract has been made for the sale of the car for $350. If she does not accept the counter-offer, then some new offer would have to be made by one of them and accepted by the other. Offer and acceptance is the only way a binding agreement can be formed, and each must be clearly understood by the other.

This rule is somewhat different if one or both of the parties involved is a merchant who deals in the particular product or service involved on a regular basis. Such merchants are governed by the Uniform Commercial Code, under which in certain cases an acceptance that alters the original terms of the offer may be held to be valid, so long as both parties have acted in good faith. Once made, a contract cannot be further modified without further consideration by both parties.

If I offer to sell you my car for $100 and you accept the offer, we would normally have a contract. However, let us suppose I have two cars, and each of us was confused as to which automobile was actually being sold. Because there was not a clear understanding of what was being sold, there would be no contract. We were not mutually assenting to the same thing when we thought we had agreed that you could have the car for $100.

Withdrawal. The offeror may withdraw his offer, and this withdrawal will operate to terminate the offer, provided that the revocation was communicated to the offeree prior to the offeree's acceptance thereof. If, for example, Mr. Frigid offers Herman five dollars to shovel his driveway, and Herman accepts the offer by performance, by shoveling out the winding driveway, Mr. Frigid cannot thereafter withdraw his offer to pay Herman. He could have withdrawn the offer prior to the commencement of Herman's work, but once Herman began to shovel, he was giving value and was entitled to his pay. If Herman were told to cease shoveling in the middle of his work, he would be entitled to the fair market value of the work he had performed to the point of termination. Where performance of the requested act will often constitute acceptance, the revocation by the offeror must be tendered to the offeree prior to the commencement of his performance.

Time. Time is the other great toller that will operate to terminate an offer. Specific time periods are often expressed at the time of the making of the offer (that it will stay open for a certain length of time). At the expiration of that stated time, the offer is automatically revoked. In another instance, where time is not specifically mentioned, the passage of a reasonable period of time will operate to cancel an offer. On a more permanent basis, Father Time may take the life or sanity of the offeror subsequent to his offer. Any of these time conditions will obviate an offer originally made in good faith that could have been accepted to form a valid contract had not the intervention of time resulted in the revocation of the offer.

TYPES OF REVOCATION

Some contracts are revoked even where there has been a valid offer and acceptance and where consideration has been exchanged.

Many contracts are for personal services. Let us say that Linda contracts with Cinda for Cinda to paint a portrait of Linda. Cinda's unique talents as an artist were part of the reason Linda hired her to do the portrait. Now suppose Cinda becomes ill or otherwise does not wish to do the painting. A person cannot be compelled to perform a personal service against her wishes, because there would be no way to enforce the quality of her performance. If Cinda said she was too ill to paint Linda's portrait the contract would probably be unenforceable. Note, however, that Cinda might not be allowed to go off and paint someone else's portrait the next day. The failure to perform on the contract would have to be for a valid reason such as death or legitimate illness which would prevent performance. If Cinda simply didn't feel like painting Linda's portrait and attempted to paint Sarah instead, then Linda could attempt to get a temporary restraining order preventing Cinda from painting anyone at all for the length of the contract's intended duration; but Linda could not force Cinda to paint her. This problem often crops up among performers. A singer may have a contract to sing in a small town and suddenly develop laryngitis, only to show up on the scheduled night at Madison Square Garden. Because the performer was contracted to appear in the small town, the town promotors would not be able to compel him to appear there because his singing is a personal service, but they could restrain him from performing in New York.

The same rule of law would apply if you contracted with someone to paint your house. If at the appointed time the painter decided to take another job that would pay him twice as much, you would not be able to compel him to paint your house, but you might be able to stop him from painting any other house during the time he was supposed to be working for you, and you might be entitled in addition to recover from him any extra money over the original contract price it cost you to have your home painted subsequently by another painter. The reasoning is that the extra costs incurred by you in having to hire another painter were the *natural and probable consequences* of the breached contract by the original painter. This rule is also applicable if a workman walks off the job and you are forced to hire another laborer to complete the work at an increased price to you. You would be entitled to recover an amount sufficient to put you in the position you *would have been in* had the contract been completely performed.

Destruction of Subject Matter
The destruction of the subject matter of the contract will likewise operate to obviate the contract. If you hire the VFW hall for your son's wedding, as many people auspiciously do, and the hall burns down the week before the occasion, then the subject and purpose of the transaction has been destroyed, and there would be no way the contract could practically be enforced.

Frustration of Purpose
And Impossibility of Performance
In other instances, the purpose for which a contract was made may become frustrated, or one party may no longer be able to use the performance or service of the other party. For example, suppose you had rented a room on an offshore island, only to discover that there was an epidemic on the island and that the health authorities advised against coming to the island. The purpose for your contract would have been frustrated, and you would probably be entitled as a result to a refund of your money. Contrarily, there are people every year who rent hotel rooms in Green Bay, Wisconsin, a year in advance of the Super Bowl with the hopes that the Packers will be involved therein. Assuming that the Packers are not participants in the Super Bowl, are the loyal fans who rented those rooms back in April entitled to a refund of their money on the theory of frustration of purpose? Probably not, because in that case they *assumed the risk* that the Packers might not be involved, and it was recognizably and in advance a substantial risk they willingly took. Meanwhile, the hotel had reserved the rooms and turned away

other customers who otherwise would have paid money for the rooms had they been listed as available. It would be unfair to compel that hotel to refund money to which it otherwise would have been entitled. This is clearly distinguishable from the unforeseen risk in an epidemic or even the cancellation of a regularly scheduled event.

PAROLE EVIDENCE

As previously discussed, the greatest cause for disputes in contract revolve around reliably proving the contents of the contract, if in fact there was a contract. The world where a man's word was his bond is fast disintegrating. Therefore, it makes the best sense to get your contract in writing and have that writing contain every element of your agreement.

A very important rule of evidence, the *parole evidence rule*, says that when two or more parties enter into a contract in writing, the resulting written instrument operates as the complete and final expression of their agreement. Any other promises or agreements made orally would be immaterial. The courts assume under this parole evidence rule that once you have committed an agreement to writing, all parties have expressed their wishes completely. These written terms cannot then be contradicted by oral testimony except in rare circumstances.

This rule of contracts is the nexus between most disputes. The carpenter who tells you not to worry because he will use genuine Formica for your kitchen should put that assertion in writing. What if you later discover that he used an imitation? Unless the contract specifically said that brand, your attempts to prove his promise to use Formica may be inadmissible as evidence.

If you are purchasing a home and the sellers tell you that they will include their washer–dryer combination and the carpeting as parts of the purchase, that promise is unenforceable unless it is put in writing, generally as part of the purchase and sale agreement for the home.

Without multiple witnesses or written evidence it becomes extraordinarily *difficult to prove* an agreement that is not in writing. "But we shook on it!" does not an airtight case make, irrespective of one's reputation in the community for honor and integrity. Oral contracts are as valid as written contracts, *but try to prove it*. It is therefore always wisest to reduce all agreements to writing.

The Writing as Protection

In short, do not be led astray by promises of good will or of personal word. Many parties to contracts tend to intimidate or embarrass the other party away from *insisting* that every term of the agreement be in writing. Do not be so intimidated. If the other party means what he promises and has full intentions of standing behind his word, he should have no objection to placing his assertions and terms in writing as a part of the total agreement.

If the woman who cleans your sewer line tells you that as part of the contract her work is guaranteed for ten years, check to see that those words are a part of the contract. If she tells you it's not there, but that she has stood behind her work for thirty years, insist nonetheless that she put it down in writing. If she really does stand behind her work, what would she have to lose? If her word is just so much puffery designed to get you to award her the contract without her having to commit herself to a written guarantee, look what you will have gained by having the full text of the agreement in writing. Two years later, should your sewer line back up, it will be the difference between her being legally bound to repair the line again at no charge or your having to pay a thousand dollars more to someone else because she denies ever making such a lengthy guarantee and takes out the contract to show that no such guarantee was made a part thereof.

Oral assurances in contracts for home insulation is a new area of contention in written contracts. Buyers should insist not only that the price and work description be in writing but also that the grade (known as the R-value), type, and brand of insulation be included in the contract. The number of home insulating firms doubled in 1977 from 1976, and consumer agencies are flooded with complaints from unwary homeowners who failed to get all the specifications and alleged guarantees into a clear writing. They are left without legal resource because the written contract failed to specify the quality and characteristics of the material.

Inclusion of All Terms. Let us suppose that you contract to build a home. You decide on what you want in the house and a price for it all. But as the contract is being written up the built-in dishwasher you discussed is omitted. When it's time to move in, you notice there is no dishwasher. Must the builder install the appliance as promised? Under the parole evidence rule, not only does he not have to, but statements reflecting his promise would be inadmissible in a court of law. The written contract was intended by the parties to be the complete expression of their agreement, and the prior oral promise would only vary the terms of the written agreement. If you wanted the dishwasher, it was your responsibility to be certain it was a term of the contract and not the mere assurance of the builder.

Of course, parties to the contract must have had the intention that the contract was to be the final expression of their mutual agreement. If the written agreement is not complete, the entire contract may be held to be oral. And should the contract have been made illegally or fraudulently, or if there were some basic misunderstanding or ambiguity under which the contract was mistakenly signed (not just an omission), then the parole evidence rule would not preclude oral testimony from being allowed to rectify the wrong.

Also, any subsequent oral agreements made after the

written instrument was executed which contradict that instrument will not be excluded from being admissible as evidence. But these are rare exceptions, and it is still better to get even these subsequent oral agreements in writing.

Mandatory Writings (Statute of Frauds)

It should also be noted that under various regulations, certain contracts *must* be in writing or they are unenforceable, irrespective of any oral assurances. The purchase and sale of land, stocks, bonds, and security agreements must be evidenced by a contract or some other integration of writings. These writings can be valid as a contract, even if they need to be pieced together and are informal notes, letters, agreements, or receipts, but they must be in writing. Generally designated as the "statute of frauds," the requirement of some kind of writing, memorandum, or note signed by the party incurring the obligation that at least identifies the parties and contains the basic terms of the agreement is also applicable to contracts that will extend beyond a year; leases for over one year; the sale of goods over $500; and the creation of an agency, executor, or guarantor relationship.

VOIDABLE AND UNENFORCEABLE CONTRACTS

Contracts made under certain circumstances may be held to be voidable. A contract is voidable when a party who for certain exceptions cited hereafter does not have the capacity or power to be bound under a contract nonetheless enters into one. This party may later choose to obviate that contract and have it declared unenforceable. Or, at his option, he may choose to go ahead and honor the contract. The contract then may be valid or it may be voided at the option of the party the law seeks to protect. So we say the contract is voidable or void only if that election is made.

Minors

The most notable group lacking the capacity to be bound to a contract are minors. The age of minority varies among states, but usually lies between the ages of eighteen and twenty-one.

Let us suppose that your sixteen-year-old daughter purchases a used car. She gets home and, after a rational chat with you that includes the assurance to you that she will be paying for the car in full, she decides it would be better to return the vehicle from whence it came. She tries to do just that, but is stopped at the driveway of Eunice's Used Car Emporium by Eunice herself, armed with the sales contract signed by your impetuous child.

Fortunately, the law has provided for the rashness and folly of our youth. A contract by an infant (anyone under the age of majority) is voidable at the option of the infant. This is true even if, for example, your daughter has misrepresented her age to Eunice, claiming to be twenty-one.

Although a contract made by an infant is voidable by the infant, it is voidable by the infant only. The party of majority age is bound to that contract as if both parties were of equal capacity. If after Eunice sold your daughter the car Eunice discovered she has a buyer willing to pay a hundred dollars more for it, Eunice could not cancel the contract on the grounds that your daughter was a minor and therefore there was no binding contract.

Although the infant at his option may void the contract, he must, in most states, return the goods that he has gained from the contract upon his disaffirmation. If the goods are lost or used up, restitution will not be required. Your daughter could not stop all payments on the car she bought from Eunice and still keep the car. (It should be noted that a minor cannot be held to have disaffirmed contracts involving real estate until he reaches the age of majority).

If a minor conveys property to a buyer, he can void that conveyance at any time up to the age of majority. In some states, the minor cannot void the real estate contract *until* he reaches the age of majority. Even subsequent bona fide purchasers of the property will have to surrender title to the property if the minor exercises his rights years later.

Where the minor contracts for goods that are "necessaries" of life, such as food or basic clothing, minors may void these contracts, but the "fair market value" for these goods likewise must be rendered or the goods returned. If the infant has a parent who will supply his necessities, then he has no right to contract for them and the contract would be voidable.

Drunk or Insane

Contracts made by people who are intoxicated and people who are legally insane are also voidable at the option of those parties, but they are liable for any necessaries they may have contracted for. Contracts negotiated by certain unauthorized corporate officers may also be voidable, but their making is relatively rare.

Illegal Contracts

Illegal contracts are *void*, which means they are unenforceable in any way and no party can sue for their breach. Even if one party has performed, he cannot recover restitution for his performance. Thus, if your bookie fails to pay you for your winning bet, you cannot sue him in a court of law for breach of contract. Your claim against a hitman whom you paid in advance or against a lady of the night whom you paid in advance is unenforceable. Massachusetts has an odd law, one of its infamous "Blue Laws," that makes any contract made on a Sunday illegal; though this law soon may be passé, it has provided numerous shrewd dealers with a way out of the oven. Promises to marry are unenforceable in most states, even if they are in writing.

Fraud

Oftentimes contracts are induced by *fraud*, which is the knowingly false concealment of a pertinent fact with the express intent of having the other party rely on the resulting misimpression. For example, if Oscar tells Martha that the Ford he is trying to sell her has a new transmission, when in fact the transmission is ten years old, and Martha buys that car relying on Oscar's assurances, then the contract for the sale of that vehicle may be voided by Martha. If the fraudulent act causes actual damage, the defrauded party may be able to obtain restitution for the actual harm created by the fraud.

A *fraudulent* contract is a contract that is not the one the defrauded party understood he was entering. It is voidable (not void) and may thus not be enforced against the party who was defrauded. If Robin is induced to buy a new typewriter and later discovers that the typewriter is used, she may at her option void the contract by returning the typewriter and get her money back.

Duress

Contracts entered into under the threat of physical violence are voidable, as are contracts induced by the use of a confidential relationship. Such unenforceable contracts are deemed to have been induced unconscionably. If you are the victim of such foul play, you should be able to avoid contractual obligation.

Separating Legal from Illegal

Some contracts may be found to be legal in parts and illegal in others. In such cases the entire contract will not be declared illegal. Rather, the legal sections will be separated and enforced, while the illegal ones will be severed from the contract. If the illegal parts cannot be severed without destroy-

ing the entire contract, then the entire contract will probably
be held to be unenforceable.

THIRD PARTY CONTRACTS

There are several other types of valid contractual relation-
ships, such as third-party beneficiary contracts (a contract
made between two parties for the benefit of a third party);
assignments (giving to a third party the rights and benefits
possessed by one of the original parties to a contract); and
suretyship (a contractual promise to answer to the duties of
another). As these are relatively complex, a lawyer should be
consulted in most cases before you enter into any such
agreement.

Such agreements are not easily understandable by the
layman. If, for example, a friend asks you to co-sign on a
note with him—as a formality—you should recognize that
you are about to enter into a complex contractual agreement
for which you should get legal advice. It is no mere formality.
You may in fact be held fully liable for a note you co-sign if
the primary signator defaults on the payments.

MEASURE OF DAMAGES

When a party to a contract seeks ordinary damages from the
other party for *breach* of contract, he asks the courts to place
him in a position he would have been in had the contract
been fully performed. The injury he has suffered determines the amount of his recovery. However, the injured
party cannot increase his damages by continuing to perform
after the other party breaches and thereby causing more
expense.

The party seeking damages is suing on the existing contract for a failure of another party to perform. To repeat, the goal of suing for damages is to place the parties to the contract in a position as if the contract had been fully performed. If there has been only a partial breach, suit may be instituted for those damages caused by the partial breach.

A party who is the victim of a total breach of contract may wish instead to seek restitution instead of damages. Restitution says that the contract is cancelled and seeks to place the parties to it in the position they were in before the contract was made. It would dictate, for example, the return of goods that had previously been paid for.

Where the injury is minimal, the injured party will be able to obtain only nominal damages. If the damages are set forth in advance in the contract, however, such *liquidating damages* will be fully enforced unless they are unconscionable. But remember that the breach must be considered *material*—going to the very heart and essence of the contract's intent—before the courts can permit a party to consider a contract as breached. If the bulk of the contract terms have been met, a minor breach will not operate to void or nullify the contract.

In certain rare cases, the breaching party may be ordered to *specifically perform* the contract as originally promised. This remedy is not used very often, because of the difficulties inherent in forcing someone to perform satisfactorily. Only where money damages are inadequate, as in the case of real estate or a unique personal item like a Renoir painting, would an aggrieved party seek specific performance. The better election is to rescind the contract and seek restitution, or affirm the contract and seek damages.

Where the breach by the defendant results in further damages that are a direct consequence of that breach, the aggrieved party may also recover for these. For example, if the defendant failed to reline the brakes of the plaintiff's auto as promised, and the defendant as a result smashes into a fence, the defendant mechanic would be held liable for the damage to the car as well as for failing to repair the brakes as contracted. The accident was a direct consequence of his contractual breach.

As discussed under contracts for services, the plaintiff is entitled to the fair market value of the services he rendered up to the breach. If a service person breaches, then the measure of damages again is the amount required to put the plaintiff in the position he would have been in had the contract been fully performed. A house painter who contracts to paint your home for a thousand dollars and quits in the middle would be liable for however much money it cost you to complete the paint job, even if that amount exceeded a thousand dollars.

CONTRACTS THAT AREN'T REALLY CONTRACTS

Promissory Estoppel

Sometimes, the courts will construe the presence of a contract even though a necessary condition is lacking, usually either consideration or mutual assent. If someone has relied upon a promise to his detriment and has given up something in reliance upon that promise, the courts under a doctrine known as *quasi-contract* or *promissory estoppel* will substitute that incurred detriment for the requirement of consideration or assent.

Such a contract is imposed by the court to prevent the unjust enrichment of one party at the expense of the other. Judgment is given to the aggrieved party for the reasonable value of the services he performed. The courts do not condone making gains in exchange for nothing of value.

A prime example of quasi-contract was just discussed in connection with voidable contracts. A minor may be held liable for "necessaries" furnished him even though he disaffirms the contract and may not be bound to it as a contract.

The aggrieved party who provided these necessaries could sue in quasi-contract. Although no actual contract had been made, the courts would create one because of the detriment incurred.

Stated another way, the law will enforce a promise as long as the person to whom the promise was made honestly believed the promise and relied on it to his detriment. Neither party can expect to be put in a better condition than he would have been prior to the reliance.

RULES OF THUMB

It is always advisable to have an attorney draft or at least examine any contract you enter into. Certainly, any contract exceeding $500 in real or potential value demands consultation with a lawyer. The insurance against omissions or improperly drafted agreements is well worth a moderate fee (usually ascertainable in advance) to a lawyer to draft a contract or to examine what you have drafted. He is trained to spot and avoid potential troublespots that would generally go unnoticed by the layman. In the end, a professional judgment may save you an enormous amount of expense, aggravation, and time spent in litigating a breach of contract action.

- Get every term in writing. Oral contracts are valid, but too often impossible to prove.
- Keep carbon copies of all communications.
- Be sure the promises are supported by consideration.
- Check to see that the party has the capacity to contract.
- Be sure seasonably to reject or accept a valid offer.

2

Landlord-Tenant Law

If you currently live in an apartment or are in the process of looking for one, you are a member of the overwhelming majority of the population who will at one time or another be classified as renters. You are, or will be, paying someone else a monthly or periodic sum in exchange for the use and occupancy of a particular premises.

There are as many reasons that a person chooses to rent rather than own a home as there are individual renters. The most common usually reflect a person's interests, commitments, and life-style, at that particular time in his life. For example, renting affords the individual a greater degree of mobility; it is far easier to leave an apartment as whim or necessity may dictate than to sell and vacate an entire house.

There is also much less responsibility in renting an apartment; the landlord handles all the repairs and improvements, and in the process absorbs the accompanying headaches. There are no unanticipated or critical expenses for the renter; his monthly rent is fixed and relatively steady. He does not have to worry about the burdens of insurance, except pertaining to his personal property, which in most instances is minimal. Neighborhood deterioration, taxes, natural disasters, and the feeling of being interminably stuck in one place are problems to which the renter does not have to look forward.

FINDING AN APARTMENT

Most people look for an apartment by going through a rental agent. The favorite ploy of the rental agent may be to show the prospective tenant four or five dreadful apartments and wear him out in the process. Then, the tired searcher is confronted with apartment number six, which is only adequate at best, but looks like a castle in comparison with the other listings.

The place may have a cracked kitchen window, a hole in the bedroom wall, and no security lock; but the agent says the landlord usually fixes those things up before the tenant actually moves in and not to worry about it. Thinking it's by far the best thing he's seen all day (and it is!), the tenant goes back to the rental office in the agent's car and immediately signs a lease for occupancy to become effective on the first day of the following month. The agent shakes his hand and tells him what a pleasure it was to meet him and that if he ever has any problems, not to hesitate to call. It is the last time the new, officially contracted tenant will ever see the rental agent. The odds are overwhelming that the agent has never even met the principal who is the new landlord.

Price

Before you begin the search for an apartment, you should develop a realistic portrait of what you and the market can mutually afford, as well as what exactly you consider essential in your apartment. If your expectations are not born of fantasies, do not deviate significantly from that standard, no matter what an agent shows you.

For example, have a definite price range in mind. It's probably going to be one of the first questions the agent asks you. Have a figure prepared that includes not only a base rent but also any utilities payments you might be obligated for. A preliminary check with the local utility companies will provide you with base rates that, according to your habits, you can adjust in order to approximate a monthly average.

The rental agent should be able to tell you which utilities are not included in the rent. Don't rely on his estimation of how much they might cost each month; he doesn't make his money by reading the meters. If you are apartment-hunting where winters tend to be chilly and last several months, be cautious if you will be responsible for the heating bill or will be "sharing" the heating bill with other tenants in the building. The icy condition of your bank account after one winter will long remind you of an oversight.

After you have told the agent approximately what you are willing to spend on this apartment that he is going to find you, he will probably give you the "for just a few dollars more" pitch. Those few dollars more, however, can quickly become *many* dollars more if you unwisely succumb to such temptations as a fireplace (which may not work), a view, wall-to-wall carpeting and the like. If such luxuries as a dishwasher, a garbage disposal, an in-house TV antenna, or a person at the front desk who screens your visitors are important features in your apartment, you are going to pay for them. Any rental agent is going to be more than pleased if you lack will power. Remain realistic about what you can afford, irrespective of whatever your agent or your younger sister thinks may suit your personality.

Also, you will find that two identical apartments in the same building will vary in price. For a few dollars less you may be able to get the first-floor apartment, instead of the third-floor unit; however, the third-floor apartment was not flooded last spring, and the first-floor apartment may not have windows above ground level. The fifth-floor apartment may be ten dollars cheaper than the second floor unit, but only because the building does not have an elevator. If you're being shown an apartment in a large, modern building, consider why the apartment next to the trash chute is somehow almost always available.

Condition

Once you are shown an apartment that interests you, inspect the premises carefully. Check to be certain that the refrigerator and stove are in working order. If they are not, the chances are excellent that they were not working when the previous tenants vacated; and nobody goes without a refrigerator or a stove by his own choice. Also check to see what kind of closets and cupboard space exists. Check for items that are peculiar to seasonal use, such as storm windows. These windows may not be there in August when you sign the lease—and they may not be there in December. All these things will affect your comfort in your apartment, and they also may indicate some very important things about your landlord.

Look for old insect traps, boric acid crystals, or other devices that might hint at an unexpected but constant source of unwelcome roommates. Ask the agent whether or not the building has ever been plagued with roaches, rats, or mice. If his reply is an unequivocal negative, insist that he state the same directly in the lease. If you subsequently learn that the problem has existed in the building for years, you may have a cause to move out of the apartment on the grounds that the landlord—through his authorized agent—substantially misrepresented a material fact, thereby ending your obligations under the lease. If you cannot get a definite answer from the rental agent or if the building is an old one, insist that it be

written into the lease that exterminator service be supplied
by the landlord on a regular basis.

Examine the locks, doors, and windows for evidence of
recent burglaries. Many unsafe buildings, particularly in
urban centers, have a high rate of transient occupancy because of break-ins in the building. As they become harder to
rent, the units in that building are rented for less, to a point
where upon superficial examination they appear to be good
values. If there is a new lock or door in the apartment, ask
about the crime problem. If you are considering a ground-
floor or basement apartment, check to see what kind of burglar protection the windows have and, depending on the
reputation of the neighborhood, request a police lock on the
door. The agent or landlord cannot legally lie to you about
something as material as the safety of the building. A lease
executed by you while material facts were fraudulently al-
tered or misrepresented may void a lease.

Precautions. If possible, you should view the apartment
with another person, preferably not someone who will be
living in it with you. Not only can this other person offer an
objective set of opinions not generated out of the pressures
you are under, but she can also be a disinterested witness to
the condition of the apartment at the time you saw it and to
the statements and assurances made by the landlord or his
agent.

It is also an excellent idea to try to talk with the present
occupants of the apartment if they are still living in the unit.
Often, the quarters are shown during the day when the current residents are working or at school. In this case, be sure
to note their names on your way out past the mailbox and
give them a call that night. You might be enlightened, if not
amazed, to discover why they have chosen to vacate that
apartment. If the apartment is vacant, return to the building
around dinnertime that evening. You will get a better idea of
the character and noise level of the neighborhood, and one

of the returning residents of the building may be happy to discuss the tribulations and rewards of living in that particular building.

Even a big gambler sizes up the players and the layout before he sits down at the table. To move into a new apartment without taking precautions is far worse than a gamble; and it would be due only to luck if you proved to be happy in a place you never checked up on.

Most important, that lease you sign is a contract in the strictest sense of the word. When you sign it, you are agreeing to each and every term stated therein. Any later cries of "I just naturally assumed . . . ," will fall on deaf ears. Likewise, if your requests and demands are not made a part of that agreement and you do not see your clauses typed into the lease, you will have no recourse for enforcement of your provisions. Make sure you witness that the agent or landlord signs the lease; if he doesn't sign it, it is not a contract.

Make a List

If you decide that the apartment is right for you, you should list the defects in the apartment and anything that you were promised would be added to the apartment. Needed repair and promised additions should be included in the lease. That way, if the kitchen sink has not been repaired by the time you move in or the new refrigerator you were promised hasn't been delivered, the landlord will be breaching his contractual obligations under the lease. Damages to the premises, such as the hole in the bedroom wall, should be noted so that you will not later be held responsible and be charged for them when it's time to regain your security deposit.

The list should be prepared in duplicate and signed by you and the landlord or his agent. Each party to the agreement should keep a signed copy of this list for possible evidence later on. If the landlord refuses to subscribe to this list, don't take the apartment. Either he is going to hold you responsible for existing damages at a later date or he does not intend to fix anything that is faulty. If he is honest, he has nothing to lose by signing the list; you have a great deal to lose if he doesn't.

If certain existing defects do not become evident until you move in, notify your landlord in writing (keeping a carbon for yourself) of the damage. Send it to him by certified mail, to give you proof that the letter was sent, and keep the return receipt.

Security Deposits
It would perhaps be more equitable if landlords gave their tenants security deposits to insure that all requested repairs would be made promptly and in accordance with the lease. However, the standard arrangement is for the tenant to give the landlord a certain sum of money as security for the rent and for any damage that the lessee or tenant causes to the property. The average security deposit is equal to one month's rent, but some landlords require more than that. Many states and local laws prohibit the landlord from assessing a security deposit in excess of two months' rent; it is certainly inadvisable under any circumstances for a tenant to entrust a landlord with more than the equivalent of two months' rent.

A few states have adopted laws that require landlords to pay interest on security deposits. Massachusetts, for example, requires the landlord to pay interest at five percent on any deposit held for a year or longer. Check the local laws, because in some areas tenants may be entitled to collect this interest before the termination of their tenancies.

Even if no damage has been done to the apartment and the landlord is in receipt of the rent due him, he still may refuse to return the security deposit. Many landlords make a good deal of extra money on the too-often correct assumption that the average layperson does not possess either the resources or a sufficient knowledge of his rights to sue in court for the money tendered as a security deposit.

There is no reason that a tenant should not demand the return of this money unless he still owes rent or actually did substantial damage to the apartment beyond normal wear and tear for the time he resided in the apartment. For example, a landlord who claims that he is holding $100 of the security deposit to clean the rugs would probably lose in court if the tenant had resided in the apartment for five years. The landlord must allow for normal usage of the unit. The same rule would apply for painting the apartment after several years of occupancy.

Other landlords will try to charge for damage that existed in the apartment before the present tenancy. If the tenant did not make the list suggested earlier in this chapter, it will be his word in court against the landlord's. The landlord generally has greater credibility than the tenant, who is offering self-serving and basically unprovable testimony. If the tenant holds a description of the defects and a dated postal receipt corresponding to the date on the list, the landlord will be hard-pressed to prove his case and probably will be ordered to return the security deposit in full.

Regaining the Deposit. Often justifiably suspicious of their landlords, many tenants assume the initiative in the battle for the security deposit and withhold the final month's rent, instructing the landlord to apply the security deposit as the final term's rent. There may be certain difficulties with this approach. If the landlord is holding more than the equivalent of one month's rent, he will still have an excess. Also, if the state in question allows interest on the deposit, the tenant likely will be forfeiting that interest by instructing the landlord to keep the security deposit.

Another approach for the tenant is to call the landlord, inform him that the apartment is being vacated, and arrange for the landlord to inspect the premises in the presence of the tenant and a witness. The tenant should insist that the landlord specify any damage he will be claiming the tenant caused and the amount he will deduct from the security deposit. The landlord should be challenged if he is inaccurate and should be sued in court if the tenant remains dissatisfied with the outcome of the inspection or the landlord's assessment of damages.

If the landlord does not agree to this inspection, then the tenant and his witness (the same witness who inspected the premises before the tenant moved in, if possible) should make a thorough list of the damages to the premises and should take photographs, if possible, prior to vacating the premises.

The landlord should return the security deposit by the time the tenant is ready to move out. Some states provide the tenant with extraordinary remedies, such as a right to twice the amount of money originally due, if the landlord does not promptly refund the security deposit. Small claims courts and night courts are simple and accessible vehicles that can be utilized by laypeople to assert their rights in matters of this kind. Timidity may be what the landlord is hoping for. If there has been no real damage, the tenant should insist on a full refund of the deposit.

TENANTS UNDER A LEASE

In most states there are two major types of tenancies, lease and nonlease. (Less common is the *tenant at sufferance*, who is something like a trespasser and whose rent is determined by the fair market value of the premises.) The first and most common tenancy is one with a lease, also known as a tenancy for years. An agreement is drawn up in writing between the tenant and the landlord that permits the tenant to occupy a specified dwelling place for a certain period of time and for a certain sum of money (rent). This agreement is known as a lease; and as a contract, it follows all the rules discussed earlier in the chapter on contracts.

As a binding contract, the lease holds the tenant in an apartment for a term of months—usually one or two years—and the landlord may not force the tenant out or alter the terms of this tenancy while that contract is in effect. Among other things, during the time of the agreed tenancy, the rent cannot be raised.

Many landlords send the residents of their buildings notices of a rent increase. Those without leases may be required either to pay the increase or to vacate the premises; those with leases do not have to do either. They are fully protected under the laws of contract from any alterations in the agreement. Once the lease expires, the terms may be changed, depending upon local and state regulations.

As tedious as it may appear to be and as much as you may trust your rental agent, be sure to read each provision in the lease. The rental agent and the landlord know what the restrictions are, as they drew up that lease to protect themselves. Your ignorance of a condition stated in the lease and to which you have agreed by signing that lease is not going to excuse your being bound by it.

Tax Escalator Clauses

An increasing number of leases today contain a clause, usually placed at the beginning of the agreement, known as the tax escalator clause. If agreed to, this provision allows the landlord to charge any increased taxes on his property to the tenants of that property on a proportional basis.

The tenants do not have to share any increase ever assessed to the landlord from the time he bought the building. Each lease must contain a base year from which increases are measured; tenants agree only to pay increases commencing with the base year stated in the lease clause. Many landlords try to insert as the base year a date of several years past when taxes were significantly lower. If that old date is agreed to, the tenant will be bound to pay the landlord his proportionate share of the difference between whatever the taxes were back then and the current assessment.

A typical tax escalation clause would be as follows:

> It is agreed that in any tax year commencing with the year 1974 for which the real estate taxes on the land and buildings of which the leased premises are a part are in excess of the amount of the real estate taxes thereon for the year 1973, the Lessees will pay to the Lessor as additional rent hereunder, when and as designated by notice in writing by the Lessor, 50% (fifty percent) of such excess that may occur in each year of the term of this lease or any extension or renewal thereof and proportionately for any part of a calendar year. Notwithstanding anything contained herein to the contrary, the Lessees shall be obligated to pay only that proportion of such increased tax as the unit leased by them bears to the whole of the real estate so taxed, and if the Lessor obtains an abatement of the real estate tax levied on the whole of the real estate of which the unit leased by the Lessees is a part, a proportionate share of such abatement, less reasonable attorney's fees, if any, shall be refunded to said Lessees.

The tenant is obligated under this clause to tender only the proportion of the tax increase that his dwelling space bears to the whole of the real estate being taxed. If taxes increase two hundred dollars on a four-unit building in which each unit is the same size, each tenant would be responsible for compensating the landlord fifty dollars. The proportional division is not based on the number of tenants in the building but rather on the area of each unit.

In many states there are certain restrictions on the phrasing of these clauses. A statement that each tenant is entitled to a proportional refund or *abatement* if the taxes are lowered from the base year may be required; in its absence the entire clause may be held invalid. If the landlord fails to conform to these requirements, it may not be in your best interests to inform him of his error. If the clause is left improperly written, the landlord may be denied his right to collect the increase.

Prior to paying any increase, the tenant should determine from the local assessor's office the exact amount of the taxes billed for the property in question, both for the base year and for the current year. This is the only way to determine accurately if the charge levied in ostensible accordance with the tax escalation clause is honest and accurate.

Penalty Clause

Many leases contain a clause that mandates a penalty if the tenant is late in his payment of rent. A large number of states have declared that this penalty money is illegal unless the rent is more than thirty days late. Whereas most of these clauses provide for a penalty if the rent is six days overdue, it is unwise for a tenant to pay the penalty without first checking to see if such a clause is legal in his state and what restrictions may exist in the exercise of that clause.

The rental period and the date rent is due are defined in the lease. Usually, rent is due on the first day of each month. It is not a sound practice to be consistently late in the payment of rent; if a tenant is fourteen days late in his payment, the landlord in many jurisdictions can commence eviction proceedings. Additionally, tenants who are late every month may find the landlord unwilling to let them remain on the property past the period of the lease term.

Your Rights as a Lessee

The most important characteristic of a lease tenancy is that the tenant is given a property right in a named rented premises. In effect, he retains exclusive possession of a specific premises for a certain length of time. Although the landlord may own the building and the land thereon, the tenant has exclusive possession of his own unit or apartment.

The landlord cannot tell you whom you may invite to your apartment or when. He doesn't have the right to burst into your apartment unannounced at three in the morning. Under most leases, the landlord can enter the apartment periodically to inspect the premises, to make necessary repairs, or to show the apartment to a prospective tenant. Even for one of these contingencies, the landlord must give his existing tenants reasonable advance notice of the date and time of the anticipated entry. If the time is inconvenient or unreasonable for the tenant, he is generally not required to admit the landlord.

Most areas have afforded additional rights to tenants beyond their rights of possession. For example, minimum heat and hot water requirements are in effect as parts of state sanitary or health codes and are often a part of the state statutes as well. Whatever the lease says to the contrary, the tenant cannot sign away his rights to any health code enforcement or rent control provisions that exist in his area.

Co-tenants

Particularly among students and single working people, it is common for two or more individuals to sign a lease on a shared apartment. The advantages to such an arrangement are many, including a greatly reduced rent per person over what each would be paying if he lived alone.

The problem here is that most leases require joint responsibility regarding the terms of the lease. In the exact wording of the law, each co-tenant is jointly and severally liable for the obligations of his fellow co-tenants. If one co-tenant suddenly leaves the apartment, the landlord has the right to hold the remaining tenant liable for the full amount of rent due.

The practical solution to this problem is to have a special clause inserted into the lease making each tenant liable for only a stated percentage of the monthly rent and an identical percentage of any other obligations under the lease. The co-tenant not contributing the percentage agreed in the lease will have acknowledged his indebtedness to the landlord, and the remaining tenant will not be stuck with an indebtedness for the entire rent.

Subleasing

A sublet is a written agreement between the tenant named in the lease and another person whereby that other person agrees to occupy the apartment, to be bound by the conditions and terms of the existing lease, and to return the apartment to the tenant before the expiration of the lease. In effect the original tenant is thus becoming a temporary landlord for the new sublessee.

It is imperative to grasp the principle stated here. If Colby sublets his apartment to Honora for the summer, and Honora causes a thousand dollars' damage to the apartment, the landlord's contractual relationship is still with Colby, and Colby remains responsible and primarily liable for all the damage. If Honora quietly leaves the neighborhood, Colby would not only be liable for the damages but for any of Honora's unpaid rent as well.

Colby's plaintive pleas to the landlord that Honora promised to pay the rent are for naught. If Colby can find Honora he will have the right to sue her directly for the losses he sustained by reimbursing the landlord. Whether he will ever be able to find her, hire an attorney, sue her, win, and then collect money on the judgment is dubious; such a series of legal propositions can run into a good deal of money. Additionally, if a clause in your lease specifically prohibits subletting, and you decide to sublet your apartment without the knowledge of the landlord, you not only may suffer a few surprises at the hands of the sub-lessee but most certainly will be in violation of the contract you signed.

In view of these dangers, it is advisable to avoid subletting. If Colby knows that he will be staying in the apartment only nine months, at the time of moving he should request that the landlord enter into a new lease with Honora. Landlords are often willing to do this, as it gives them better leverage over the person who is living on their premises. They will on occasion charge the departing tenant a fee for this adjustment, usually between a half month's rent and a full month's rent; but the assurance of being off the legal hook is well worth the one-time added expense. It relieves the tenant of all liability, as his lease is cancelled (and all copies should be physically destroyed). The would-be subtenant becomes the new tenant, liable for her own rent and damages.

An assignment is similar to a sublease, except that in an assignment the tenant surrenders the premises for the remainder of the lease term; and both the tenant and the assignee remain liable to the landlord for the fulfillment of all the clauses of the lease. Once again, the principle still holds that only where the landlord actually discharges the tenant from his contractual obligations can the tenant be immune from liability or responsibility. A new lease should be drawn, even if it means an additional fee.

Tips on Leases

Remember to get a signed copy of the lease from your landlord. It is the basis for any claims you might have during the course of your tenancy. Be certain that all the promises made to you are written directly into the lease. Keep accurate records of any complaints made to the landlord, preferably carbon copies of letters mailed by certified mail, return receipt requested. Telephone calls and their contents are impossible to substantiate.

Insist on the inclusion of clauses that will give you the type of flexibility and protection you need to be comfortable in your home for at least the next year or more. The only thing worse than feeling trapped in your own home is to feel trapped in an apartment in which you have no real interest beyond living out a limited but unhappy tenancy.

Above all, *read the lease*. Most leases can be intimidating documents merely because of their length and the fine print. However, included in the fine print are clauses covering every item the landlord deems important, from the tax escalator clauses to pets to parking; and your conditions and requests should be equally defined. Provisions in the document may specify that you must initial certain clauses (in addition to your signature at the end) indicating that you have read, *understood*, and *agreed* to those particular sections. This is particularly likely for what could amount to a rent increase in a tax escalator clause.

Make sure you understand the terms of the lease and that the dollar amount and dates are correct. Check to see that the landlord's signature is on the lease; if it's not, the document is not binding.

TENANCIES WITHOUT LEASES

Many tenants live in rented units without a lease. In some cases, the lease they had when they first occupied the premises has expired; but they are continuing or self-extending their tenancies under the same terms and conditions as were set forth in the lease.

A tenant without a lease, called a *tenant at will*, is responsible for tendering rent in whatever amount has been agreed upon with the landlord. Practically speaking, the landlord can raise the rent, evict the tenant, or otherwise alter the terms of the tenancy at will, provided that he gives notice to the tenant equal in time to the rental period.

Thus, if the tenant pays his rent on the fifteenth day of every month, the landlord must notify the tenant on or before the fifteenth day of the month of the changes in the tenancy, which cannot normally become effective until the fifteenth day of the following month. For example, Lloyd Landlord gives Ernest Tenant notice on February 16 that the rent is going to be increased ten dollars, effective on the next rental period. Ernest pays his rent on the fifteenth day of each month. Under most state laws, Ernest would not have to pay the increase in rent until April 15. That would allow Ernest a full month's notice before the April rental period.

Once the tenant pays the increase, he is deemed to have agreed to it and will forever after be bound to that amount as the monthly rent. If the tenant does not want to pay the increase, he can continue to pay the old rent and wait for the landlord to file or not to file for a regular eviction. The tenant may still be evicted, but it will not be the swifter eviction allowed for nonpayment of rent, because the tenant will have been paying the old rent.

The alternative is for the tenant to pay the new rent, but on the back of the check he should write, "Paid under protest and without waiving any rights I may have for a refund or a portion thereof." The insertion of such a clause is proof that the tenant did not willingly pay the increase, and he will not be bound to that increase if a court later sets it aside.

Under a tenancy at will, then, either party may terminate the tenancy by giving the other side at least one full rental period's notice. If Ernest wants to vacate the apartment on July 1, he must notify Lloyd by May 15 if he pays his rent on the fifteenth day of each month, and by June 1 if he pays his rent on the first day of each month.

Notice must be in writing and should be sent by certified mail, return receipt requested. The return receipt, together with a dated copy of the notice, will afford the party giving the notice proof positive not only of when it was sent, but of when it was received as well. If notice is not received by the landlord until June 3 for a July 1 vacancy, the landlord is entitled to rent for the month of July as well, unless he succeeds in renting the apartment by July 1 to a new tenant.

For some reason, people tend to be careless about giving proper notice. A costly and incredibly troublesome situation can develop from the tenant casually giving oral notice to his landlord with one week to go before the rent is due for the next month. It is also unfair to the landlord, who may be stuck with a vacant apartment producing no rent and costing him money nonetheless for mortgage, heat, and taxes. If a suit follows, he is only protecting his interests. Landlords endure tenants who feel no responsibility for maintaining the property, who are often consistently late in rent payment, who make demands that are occasionally unrealistic, and who bolt on them without proper notice.

Both sides of the adversary relationship between land-lord and tenant have merit, and neither generally has empathy for the plight of the other. Real estate boards on the one hand and tenant organizing committees on the other tend more to exacerbate and polarize than sincerely to bridge the gap so critical for all concerned. It is the tenants and landlords without the protections of leases who feel the most vulnerable.

EVICTION

The process of eviction varies widely from state to state. One of the features shared by all types is their tremendous expense and difficulty for all parties concerned. Landlords often attempt to frighten tenants into believing they will be tossed into the streets by sunrise the following day; and tenants try to dodge and evade the landlord for months on end, thumbing their noses at the landlord who wants to be rid of an intentional headache.

Each state has certain defined procedures that must be followed in order for the landlord to "throw out" or evict the tenant. This procedure can be expensive, and it is usually time-consuming. If the tenant resists the eviction, the process can and usually does take months. Too many tenants become overly frightened upon receiving an initial notice of eviction and make immediate plans to move without finding whether it is in fact required of them.

Some landlords erroneously attempt to take the law into their own hands, using such measures as changing the locks on the tenant's door, ordering the tenant out within twenty-four hours, and the like. Such tactics may be in violation of state criminal laws, as well as rendering the landlord potentially liable in a civil suit. Additionally, if the apartment is covered by local rent control laws, other requirements must be met before any eviction is carried out.

Even if the eviction is granted after a court hearing, most judges have the power to grant a stay of judgment for several months. Usually, a reasonable time in which to move will be granted upon request of the tenant. A two- or three-month stay is not at all unusual.

Alternatively, a judge might find in favor of the tenant, in which case the tenant will have maintained his right to remain in the apartment. Both sides have the right to request an appeal, though such requests must be made immediately after the initial hearing.

It is wise to retain an attorney whether you are the tenant or the landlord. The hearing itself can be extremely complex and nerve-racking, and both sides will want to put forward the most effective possible case. Many people fail to file a proper answer in advance of the trial or fail to show up at the trial at all; these people in effect are forfeiting their right to have their side of the story heard by an impartial judge.

There are many defenses to an eviction, such as payment of rent; an invalid termination of the tenancy; an improper or defective complaint for eviction; discrimination; or the claim that the actions of the tenant that were the basis for the eviction were valid and legal. These defenses should be raised on behalf of the aggrieved tenant where they exist; generally a lawyer can best spot these defenses and plead them effectively in defense of the rights of the tenant.

Tenants as well as landlords commit housing code violations, violations of the lease agreement, and maintain nuisances. Thus, although one side brings the initial suit, the other side may have counterclaim that would offset the claim against them. The tenant may even be able to avoid eviction by pleading and proving his counterclaim.

It is therefore incumbent upon both parties not only to retain legal counsel but to proceed in a logical and sane manner in full accordance with the law. Neither party should have the other's wishes forced down his throat without the due process of law.

RENT WITHHOLDING

Some tenants erroneously think that if the landlord is tardy in making or refuses to make necessary repairs, they can as a matter of right withhold all or a portion of their rent. This generally is not true. In those states that do permit rent withholding, the tenant must often first have the particular condition certified by an appropriate local governmental agency as dangerous or in violation of existing health or building codes. Thereafter, the landlord must be given a certain period of time, usually around a month after receiving official notice of the violation or condition, to make the required repairs. Without following the required procedures, a tenant who withholds rent on his own may be deemed by the courts to be in nonpayment of his rent and open to the landlord's right of eviction.

Tenants should not attempt to withhold rent until they have checked on the local laws. The state office of consumer affairs, the rent board, the secretary of state's office, local authorities, or local tenants' groups can provide information on the details of rent withholding. Once the tenant legally withholds rent, he then has a defense to being evicted for nonpayment of rent. But the rent must be *legally* withheld; and the tenant must first be certain he has followed the requisite local procedures before he withholds.

In many states if a landlord tries to evict a tenant for withholding rent or for any other legal action to which the tenant has a right of exercise (such as reporting health and building code violations to the authorities) he can be penalized heavily, including having to pay the attorney's fees of the aggrieved tenant. Such retaliatory evictions may be illegal in your state.

RENT CONTROL

Many areas of the country are now under "rent control." Basically, under rent control laws, base rents for every residential unit in the area are established. It is unlawful for a landlord to demand, accept, receive, or retain any more than the maximum lawful base rent once rent control has taken effect. Rents can be raised thereafter only by the permission of the rent control office, after a hearing at which the affected tenants have a right to be notified and heard in opposition.

Under rent control, maximum lawful rents are adjusted to insure the landlord a "fair net operating income." Factors used in deciding whether or not a particular unit is giving the landlord his just profit include his operating expenses, his capital improvements, the taxes he must pay, and the depreciation of the value of the apartment and the building. Many rent control offices have established arbitrary percentages for a fair net return on the landlord's investment. The difficulty is that this percentage often falls far below what will satisfy the landlord, given the risks he runs.

Under rent control in many areas, landlords were clearing such a small profit that they were unable to reinvest in the building for remodeling, repairs, and renovation. This in turn resulted in the blight and deterioration of neighborhoods under rent control. For these reasons, the City of Boston all but did away with its rent control laws six years after their establishment, and many other states and cities are reconsidering their rent control procedures.

Whatever maximum rent is allowed, tenants under a lease are bound with their landlord to honor the terms of the lease. Increases allowed under rent control apply only to those tenants not under a lease, unless the increase is an "across the board" increase for the entire area.

Evictions, individual rent increases, hearings, and most violations all fall under the aegis of the local rent control board. If the property you are concerned with is under rent control, be certain to consult that office before doing anything that will affect your interest in that property. Conformity with rent control laws where applicable is mandatory.

TIPS TO REMEMBER

- Don't be pressured into renting an apartment. Know what you are looking for and stick to your standards.
- Make sure your requests are included in the lease and that the landlord signs it.
- Read the lease to make sure you understand the conditions.
- The tenant has a property interest in his apartment.
- The tenant should make a list of all existing damages to the apartment *before* he moves in.
- All communications between landlord and tenant should be in writing and mailed by certified mail, return receipt requested.
- Get all the terms agreed to in writing. Don't take anyone's word for anything.
- The safest tenancy is a tenancy under a lease.

3

Buying and Selling A House

Few decisions in a person's life are as momentous—and frightening—as the decision to purchase a home. It is usually the largest financial commitment the individual has made to that date. It is putting down roots, making an investment, expressing a commitment to a new life-style, and becoming part of an often unfamiliar community.

There are numerous tax advantages to owning your own home. When you pay rent on an apartment, you benefit from no tax deductions unless part of your apartment is used as an office. If you own real estate, however, that very significant portion of your mortgage payment that represents interest to the bank is deductible on your tax return. In effect, the government ends up paying 30 to 40 percent of your interest for you through this credit.

Similarly, your real estate tax is deductible on your return, which means that the government in effect pays about one third of that tax for you in the form of a credit. Additional deductions are allowed for improvements and expenses incurred in the maintenance of multiple-unit dwellings. Home improvements made to a two-family home, for example, may be deductible for the one-half of the cost deemed expended on the income property. If the repairs were done on only the rental part of the property, then the entire expense may be deducted. Major improvements and repairs can be depreciated or amortized, though your accountant or attorney should be consulted to insure maximum and accurate use of the benefit.

Most people have thought a good deal about purchasing a home before they actually make contact with a realtor. However, once the serious search for a home has begun, people often buy either on impulse or out of pressure. This pressure can be internal, generated out of a desire for independence, for solitude, or for a wish to provide loved ones with the best possible environment. The pressure also can be external, coming from spouse, peer, or parental expectations and further egged on by zealous brokers who vow that a home "like this one" probably never will come up as cheap again. Over-anxious to terminate the looking as early as possible and not to let a good thing slip through open fingers, the purchaser finds that an agreement is quickly drawn and signed. As a result, many people find that what should be a happy event is an impulsive, tense, and even unhappy trap.

Other people carefully and logically select their homes, thereby minimizing the chance of their feeling "stuck" six months later. Once they decide on a home, they know the necessary steps and precautions to take to lessen the potential difficulties. It is the purpose of this chapter to allow you to function from this latter group by sensitizing you to the relatively simple procedures required for a smooth purchase of personal real estate.

REAL ESTATE LISTINGS

The majority of people look for houses by first checking their local newspapers. They generally have a good idea of the neighborhood they want to live in, based upon the character and composition of the residents, the school system, the tax rate, and other individual characteristics that make some sections of every community more desirable to some people than to others. Newspapers usually list houses by city or town, and most ads in metropolitan areas end by listing the name of the broker. Many times, the ad further will specify whether the house has been given to the broker as an "exclusive." Whether you are the buyer or the seller of a house, it is important for you to understand your relationship with the broker.

Exclusive Listings

When Seller Sam signs a contract with Broker Bill for Bill to act as the "exclusive" agent in the sale of a house, the seller is agreeing that Broker Bill alone has the right to sell the house. If another unauthorized agent or even the seller himself sells it, Broker Bill is still entitled to a commission for the sale.

This does not mean that Bill and only Bill can show the house for sale. Once Bill has the contract for an exclusive, he can then allow other agents to show the house to their clients. If a client or another agent purchases the house, the second agent will share the commission with the broker, who retains the exclusive.

Oftentimes, brokers with an exclusive listing will advertise the house for sale through trade notices that go to several other agents. Often called multiple-listing services, these lists can produce faster results than if the exclusive broker kept the listing all to himself. It affords more potential buyers the opportunity to learn about the house, and it thereby increases the chances for a sale. The exclusive broker gets half a commission, and the co-exclusive broker gets the other half.

It is wisest when selling a house to limit the amount of time your broker can retain the exclusive right to sell. Many brokers won't seriously publicize the house until they absolutely are forced to, on the theory that a full commission is better than half a commission. If Broker Bill can get the seller to sign an unlimited exclusive, then Bill will show the property only to his own clients until eventually he finds someone to buy.

Therefore, limit the term of the exclusive right to sell to no more than ninety days, which gives the broker an incentive to work hard and to work fast. Also, after going through his own list of clients, he will be encouraged to list the house with other brokers on the theory that a half a loaf is better than none. He knows that at the end of ninety days the house will otherwise become an open listing.

Open Listings

An open listing is a listing given to a number of brokers. It is the alternative to giving a broker an exclusive right to sell. The first broker who produces a buyer who is ready, willing, and able to purchase the house is entitled to a full commission. This method often produces a fast sale, because brokers will try harder when they know there's a full commission awaiting them if they find an able buyer.

On the other hand, many brokers won't invest in advertising unless they have an exclusive, on the belief that advertising an open product is a risky venture. Only exclusives are listed in the multiple-listing services, and the better brokers will advertise in local newspapers only if they have an exclusive or co-exclusive.

If You Are the Seller

If you are the seller, it is thus most advisable to give an agent an exclusive right to sell for sixty or ninety days. At the end of that time, the exclusive contract will have expired, and you should then open list the house with other brokers. The average commission ranges from five to seven percent of the price for which the house sells, and you should be wary of agents who try to charge anything over ten percent. Do not bind yourself to long-term agreements with an agent, and do not violate an agreement with a broker once it is made.

Selling the House Yourself
You do not absolutely have to list your house with a real estate broker. You can try to sell your house yourself. Most people usually do this by listing it in the newspaper and by word of mouth. If you are a good negotiator and can find an able buyer, you will have saved the commission you would otherwise have had to pay a realtor. It also eliminates at least one major outside source of pressure, the realtor.

However, it is imperative that if you are selling your own home without a broker, you are certain you have retained a lawyer who is experienced in the conveyancing of houses. If you attempt to draw any of the papers of sale yourself, you almost certainly in some way will increase the likelihood that the sale either will not go through or otherwise will be in jeopardy.

THE BINDER

Although procedures involving the purchase of real estate vary from area to area, a common initial document that binds the parties into an agreement is called a "binder." In some states, it is called an "earnest money receipt" or a "conditional offer to purchase." The binder is signed by the potential purchaser and seller when the decision is made by the buyer to purchase the property and is accompanied by a cash deposit. It evinces the potential purchaser's good faith and sincerity through his agreement to make a monetary offer on that property.

Under no circumstances should you as the buyer sign a binder that unequivocally binds you to purchase the property. The binder should at least state that all monies shall be refunded if a satisfactory purchase and sale agreement is not signed within a specified period of time, usually no more than a week. The binder may also make the deal conditional upon a satisfactory structural inspection by a builder or architect of the buyer's choice. There are any number of clauses that can be inserted into a binder agreement that will not lock in the buyer if the offer he makes is accepted.

Of course, you should not sign anything unless you are reasonably certain that the house is the one you want. The binder is evidence of good faith on the part of the purchaser of real estate, and the buyer should have an honest intent to purchase.

The amount of money that goes with the binder varies with the area. The safest rule to follow is: the less you put down, the better. Many realtors will accept a hundred dollars or less for this stage of the proceedings. More and more urban brokers are requiring as much as a thousand dollars. Your lawyer or local realtors can inform you in advance how much money would be required for the initial binder and how much will be required for the purchase and sale agreement, the formal document that will normally be executed a few days thereafter.

Contents of a Binder

The memorandum called the binder is usually a pre-printed one-page form. It contains the names and addresses of the buyers and the sellers; a brief description—usually the street address—of the property that is the subject of the purchase; a statement of both the purchase price and the deposit by the buyer; the terms of the broker's commission; and the date for the later signing of the formal purchase and sale agreement, preferably together with a statement making the binder contingent upon the signing of that purchase and sale agreement.

A receipt for a deposit by the buyer to the broker as agent for the seller in which the purchase price and street address of the property is recited will be sufficient as a binder until such time as the formal purchase and sale contract can be negotiated. If the purchase and sale agreement cannot be consummated, the money deposited under the binder is generally refundable; but in no event would the buyer's liability exceed whatever money he actually put down with the binder.

THE PURCHASE AND SALE AGREEMENT

The purchase and sale agreement is the formal contract of sale between the buyer and the seller. It is called by other names in various states, notably the land-sale contract. It includes all the terms of the sale as agreed upon by the parties to the agreement. If a particular term or item is omitted from the contract, the rights to it will be lost. Because the purchase and sale agreement is a contract, the parole evidence rule discussed in the chapter on contracts would apply. That rule, you will remember, presumes that all items agreed upon by the parties are incorporated into the subsequent written contract, and evidence of any additional terms will normally be inadmissible.

The purchase and sale agreement is generally a lengthy document, three or four pages in length. It can be drawn in such a way that its terms and clauses favor the buyer, or favor the seller, or are absolutely equitable. For this reason, among others, it is prudent to have your own lawyer examine the purchase agreement before you even contemplate signing it. Only a trained eye can readily spot the slanted clauses or omitted protections that may later turn out to give you sleep-less fits of "Why didn't I . . .?"

Contents of the Purchase and Sale Agreement

As the purchase and sale agreement is the formal contract for the sale of property, it must contain the complete story of the property and the transaction therefor. A full legal des-cription of the property, including the measurements of the boundaries of the land in each direction, should be included. You must have evidence of precisely what you are purchas-ing. This description can be copied from the deed possessed by the seller, together with the property address, the title references (also found on the deed), and the date of the last formal transfer, when the seller took possession of the prop-erty.

The agreement should, of course, be dated and contain the names and addresses of each of the parties to the con-tract. If any of the parties is married, both spouses' names should appear on the purchase and sale agreement. That way, if the seller's spouse later tries to claim a right in the property, he or she will be deemed to have sold all rights to the property in the contract for sale.

Where a corporation, a conservator, or an agent is sell-ing the property, the individual should be required to prove through certified documentation that he in fact possesses the power and authority to implement the sale and is rightfully exercising that power. This may require the production of a copy of the corporate by-laws, a vote of the board of direc-tors, a certified copy of a probate court's license to sell, or a certified copy of an appointment as a conservator. Some proof is necessary, however; never assume the party you're dealing with has the power to sell. Otherwise you may find yourself left in the street, having vacated your apartment but suddenly unable to pass papers on the new house because of an unauthorized sale.

Any light fixtures, home tools, appliances, air conditioners, draperies, or furniture that are a part of the sale must be fully described in the purchase and sale agreement. This is the greatest single cause of misunderstanding between parties to a sale, and it is totally avoidable if care is taken to list everything. Nothing should be assumed. Merely because that dining room chandelier was hanging elegantly when you examined the house initially does not necessarily mean it will be there when moving day rolls around. The sellers may claim that it was not a permanent fixture that belonged with the house.

Your only recourse if disappointed is a nasty dispute at the passing of the papers or a subsequent lawsuit, neither of which is a very pleasant alternative. An inclusive purchase and sale agreement clearly including the chandelier in the dining room, the storm windows, the venetian blinds, and the downstairs awnings eliminates the misunderstandings and spells out the duties of all parties.

Financial Requirements

Normally, ten percent of the purchase price will be required from the buyer at the signing of this agreement. (In order to obtain a mortgage, however, most banks are requiring at least twenty percent down by the time of the actual passing.) The agreement should state the purchase price for the premises, how much was paid at the signing of the binder, how much more has been paid at the signing of the purchase and sale agreement, and what balance is to be paid at the time of the delivery of the deed.

Some agreements specify that the balance of the purchase price must be paid in cash at the time of the delivery of the deed, commonly called the passing of papers. You as the seller should be certain to insist on the insertion of a clause allowing payment by certified check or bank check as well. It is unsafe and absurd to march to a passing with $50,000 in cash rolled up in the lining of your overcoat!

Timing

The time for the final passing of papers should also be specified. You should allow yourself ample time to move, giving proper notice to your landlord if you are moving out of an apartment and into the new house. If you are the seller, give yourself time enough to move into your new apartment or house. Extensions on the time for delivery of the deed can be arranged without excessive difficulty, but it is better to allow the right amount of time in the purchase and sale agreement.

It should be noted that the buyer should try his best to sell his own house prior to entering into an agreement for a new house. There are a plethora of unfortunate incidents where the buyer of a new house is forced to take any offer on his old house, often for less than what he rightfully should receive, because he needs the money to pay for his hew house. Even worse, many buyers find themselves living in their new houses and for many months thereafter paying real estate taxes, heating bills, and mortgage and interest payments on two houses. This dual ownership can be an extremely heavy loss financially for the buyer who bought too soon.

Many people want to pass papers immediately, but it takes time to prepare all the necessary papers, particularly those that pertain to the new mortgage.

The Mortgage-Financing Clause

The purchase and sale agreement *must* be made subject to the buyer's obtaining the money needed as a mortgage at the prevailing rate at the time of the agreement. This is not, however, automatically part of the agreement, and the buyer must insist upon its inclusion. Many purchase and sale agreements are pre-printed forms that do not contain this special provision. If it is a mandatory clause, one may wonder why it is omitted from that standard form. The answer may lie in the fact that many of these forms are printed by the local real estate boards for distribution to its agents. Real estate agents who prepare these forms for the buyer and the seller are naturally interested in consummating a sale once an agreement has been reached.

By insisting on a mortgage-financing contingency, you as the buyer are inserting the possibility that if you don't obtain the mortgage you need at prevailing rates, the contract will not be binding on you. Thus, the realtor may lose his commission. Real estate boards don't want this to happen, and by omitting the clause, they make it less likely that you will require it. They may succeed, unless you have wisely hired an attorney to inspect the agreement before you sign it or are otherwise versed in the protections you need to insist upon.

The pains you will suffer for not having a mortgage-financing contingency clause made part of the agreement are far worse than any temporary insecurity borne by the realtor, who at the worst will lose a fee. Do not therefore let the realtor pressure you into signing an agreement without this vital clause.

Let us suppose that you and your husband decide you love the house at 1776 Pleasant Street, and you sign a purchase and sale agreement for $50,000. You need a mortgage for $40,000, having saved up just enough on your own to put down twenty percent. Once you go to a few banks, you discover that your credit rating is not good enough for a mortgage. Perhaps neither of you has held a steady job for a long enough time; or you may have too many outstanding bills; or the bank is otherwise unwilling to trust you because of your youth or your credit, or because they feel the property you are about to purchase isn't worth the risk. Without the contingency clause, you will somehow have to come up with the $40,000 from friends, relatives, and the Lord; and the odds are against any of these entities coming up with that kind of instant money.

It is also a not uncommon occurrence for the bank to inform you that they will grant you the mortgage, but at a greatly increased rate of interest. As an illustration, a $40,000 mortgage at an annual rate of interest of nine percent held for twenty-five years will cost the mortgagor $100,704 if he keeps it for the full term. The same mortgage for the same term of years but at an increase in the rate of one percent to a rate of ten percent will cost the mortgagor $109,047. In other words, the interest differential in one percent is an astounding $8,343.

It is thus also mandatory that you insist that the mortgage must be not only obtainable, but also obtainable at the prevailing rate of interest. Otherwise, you may be compelled to accept a mortgage that is going to cost you thousands of extra dollars, merely because you didn't insert that one precautionary phrase into the contingency clause.

Shopping for a mortgage is the worst time at which to be timid, because the consequences of one-stop buying can be astronomically expensive. Too many people go directly to one bank, have their application approved, and accept the rate of interest without any comparison at all. These are usually the same people who spend ten minutes laboring over two comparable cans of peas or drive into the next town to save a penny a gallon at the bargain filling station.

Of course, the contingency clause cannot be operative indefinitely. It would be unfair for the seller to be held up for four months while the buyer attempted to produce a mortgage at a minimal rate or tried in vain to establish a good credit rating. The seller has a vested interest in a quick and a smooth sale and has a right to limit the time on the mortgage-financing contingency clause.

The seller normally should not allow the buyer more than two weeks in which to secure a mortgage. That is plenty of time for the good-faith purchaser to shop for a satisfactory bank. The seller may wish to extend the clause an additional week if there is no immediate pressure on him to move; but every additional day beyond a reasonable two-week period is time that would be better spent lining up another more likely buyer. It is a fair assumption that other potential buyers are being driven away or kept away because of the continuing tenous situation.

Normally the buyer is deemed to have waived his rights under the contingency clause if the seller has not been notified in writing by the end of the agreed-upon time limit that the buyer desires to terminate the purchase and sale agreement. It is the responsibility of the would-be buyer to notify the seller that he couldn't get a satisfactory mortgage and the purchase of the house is therefore terminated. Under normal circumstances, provided due care has been taken in the wording of the agreement, all monies tendered to the seller will then be refunded in full to the buyer.

When There Is No Broker

It is not uncommon for a buyer who initially hears about a house from a broker to approach the seller directly, without the knowledge of the broker. The buyer convinces the seller to lower his price on the grounds that the seller won't have to pay a broker's commission of thousands of dollars. The seller believes the buyer, lowers his price, sells the house, and then is slapped with a lawsuit by a real estate broker who rightly claims that he produced the buyer and is entitled to his full commission.

If the buyer has directly approached the seller without a broker or if there is no broker involved in the transaction, it will be necessary for you as the seller to insist upon the insertion in the purchase and sale agreement of a clause that will indemnify you (make you harmless) and hold the buyer responsible for any realtor's fee or commission that might be asserted in connection with that particular transaction. The provision should extend even beyond the transfer of ownership of the house, since many times it is months or even years afterwards before a broker will discover he was actually due a commission.

Similarly, all references to a broker should be meticulously deleted from the printed agreement. Note that the standard form for the agreement contains no protection for the unwary seller but only a clause providing for the broker's commission, proving once again that real estate boards are not so much interested in the protection of the public as they are the garnering of their own sometimes unethical profit.

Broker's Commission

In most instances the seller is responsible for the commission due to the broker. That commission is due to the broker at such time as he provides a buyer who is ready, willing, and able to purchase the home. However, for a multiplicity of reasons the sale might not go through; even if you as the seller are totally blameless for this failure, you might still be obligated to pay the broker his commission.

The prudent seller will insist that a clause be inserted into the purchase and sale agreement that the broker will be entitled to his commission only if the sale is consummated. The broker himself must sign the agreement in order for it to be legally binding upon him. As with all contracts, any party to be charged with a responsibility under the contract must sign the contract, or he will not be bound.

Where a commission is due, the amount should be clearly listed on the purchase and sale agreement. It will save any later dispute that might arise as a result of some troublesome misunderstanding.

Insurance

The purchase and sale agreement should provide that until the papers pass the seller should maintain at least the insurance on the property as presently insured. Some sellers, upon moving out of the house early or for some other reason, will lower their coverage to an inadequate level until the buyer takes over. Maintaining coverage of the property as normally and presently insured protects all the parties and their respective present and future interests. The buyer should, in any event, ascertain the amount of the seller's insurance; if it is inadequate, he should insist upon a specific, satisfactory amount and list that dollar amount in the body of the agreement.

It is inadvisable for the seller to assign either his insurance or his mortgage to the prospective buyer, unless documents are executed by all parties involved that fully relieve the seller from any liability whatsoever. Otherwise the seller may remain partially liable on an assignment should the buyer default on the assignment or the mortgage payments. Years after the seller has sold the property, he may find large sums of money being demanded of him by his old bank or insurance company. The best practice is for the buyer to obtain his own insurance and for the seller to cancel his insurance immediately upon the passing of title.

Additional Contingency Clauses

The mortgage-financing contingency clause is not the only contingency clause that may be inserted into the purchase and sale agreement.

The seller should insert a clause allowing him to extend the date of closing at least thirty days beyond the date named in the agreement as the time for the passing of papers. This extension is often necessary because of complexities involved in clearing the title, repairing any damage to the property, delays due to attorneys, and so on. The entire sale should not fail because of innocent or unavoidable difficulties that can be cleared up quickly. The buyer should not generally allow an extension that goes on for an uncomfortably long time, particularly if it is necessary for him to occupy the home at or near the specified date of closing.

Other contingency clauses ensure that the buyer can obtain local zoning variances or subdivision approval for the property. If the buyer cannot use the property for the purposes he intends, there is little value in his consummating the sale.

It bears repeating that where possible your attorney should examine your purchase and sale agreement before you sign it. It would be most helpful, however, if you acquire familiarity with some of the protections and clauses you will want to insist on. That way you will keep to a minimum the number of careless omissions that lead to problems on the day of the actual passing or thereafter.

SHOPPING FOR A MORTGAGE

It has already been emphasized that it is mandatory to shop for a mortgage and that your failure to do so can cost you thousands of dollars. Each bank has differing requirements and restrictions. For example, some banks charge a "point" or two, which is a euphemism for an extra fee based on a percentage of the mortgate. Usually, but not always, a point equals one percent of the mortgage amount. This point can cost you several hundred dollars and sometimes more, enough that it might be cheaper for you to use a bank that does not charge points but may have a quarter of a percent higher interest rate.

Many banks do not allow you to pay off your mortgage in full for the first several years of its term. Others don't allow you to pay lump sums or extra money over and above the regular monthly payment. You have already seen that keeping a mortgage to its full term can cost the customer two and a half times the amount he borrowed. This too is a factor to consider in choosing to which bank you will grant a mortgage.

At the beginning of the mortgage term, almost all of your monthly payment is interest; very little is applied to the reduction of the principal (the actual amount of the mortgage). If a lump-sum payment is made in a given month, however, the amount in excess of the monthly charge will be directly applied to reducing the principal; none of it is applied toward interest. Because the interest is based upon the amount of the outstanding principal, a reduced outstanding principal means that you will pay less interest. Hence it is to your advantage to pay off your mortgage as quickly as you can to reduce your interest payments, which do nothing to shorten your mortgage and only enrich the coffers of the bank. It is because so few people realize this basic principle of finance that the skyscrapers in every major U.S. city belong to the banking and insurance industries. If you doubt this fact check out your nearest urban skyline.

What the Bank Does
With Your Mortgage Application

Once you have filled out the bank's application for a mortgage, the bank's credit department will most likely examine the information you have set down as fact. They will screen your credit rating across the city, contact your employer and listed references, and ascertain whether or not you would be a safe risk as a customer.

If you pass this portion of their requirements, they will then send their building committee out to inspect the property. This committee usually is a group of people familiar with the conditions and values of houses and their neighborhoods. It is up to these people to decide whether or not the house is worth significantly more than the amount they are risking on a mortgage.

For example, if you are asking for a $40,000 mortgage on a parcel that the committee feels is worth $35,000, your mortgage application will be denied. If the home is adjudged in need of serious repair, the cost of which would lower the present value of the house to a market value below what you plan to pay for it, your application will also be denied.

On the other hand, if you are asking for a mortgage for $40,000, are putting twenty percent down, and the committee estimates the value of the house at $50,000, it is likely that your application will be approved. If you have the misfortune three months thereafter to default on the mortgage and the bank forecloses, the bank will have lost nothing. They will sell the house for a price at or near its true value, recover their full $40,000, and have plenty of additional funds remaining to pay their attorney's fees, costs of foreclosure, and administrative costs. In other words, the property must have value in excess of the bank's investment before the bank will determine that, no matter what kind of client you turn out to be, it will not stand likely to lose money.

If the above determination is made in your favor, the mortgage will probably be approved. You will receive a letter of commitment from the bank, in which the bank will assert the relevant terms of your mortgage. Generally, it is required that a swift response be made as to whether or not you plan to accept the bank's offer. This is understandable, as the bank is holding in reserve the amount of capital you requested for mortgage money. They require a quick response, telling them that you will accept their terms or that they can release that money to another party or for another purpose.

If you reject the bank's offer, then probably the only thing you will lose will be the application fee of $25 or so. If you accept it, you should immediately withdraw all other applications you have pending at other banks. Once you have accepted, the bank will turn the entire file over to one of its well-connected attorneys for a title examination and the preparation of all papers necessary for the upcoming passing. The amount of time it takes to pass papers once you have accepted the mortgage commitment varies, but count on at least a month if the bank has much financing business. In almost no event will you be living in your dream house the week after you've obtained your mortgage approval, expectations and anxieties notwithstanding.

PROCESSING THE MORTGAGE

In most parts of the country, you are not allowed to have your own attorney process your mortgage with the bank. The bank has its own attorneys, who may alternate on a rotating basis. As the customer and not the bank pays the fee for the bank attorney, many people correctly protest that they ought to have some choice of lawyer. The bank, however, argues with like merit that as it is the bank's money on the line, the bank should determine who prepares the mortgage and decides whether the property is safe from foreseeable problems. Many banks, however, are increasingly allowing the attorney of the person getting the mortgage to process the mortgage papers on behalf of the bank.

The bank attorney will himself or through a certified title examiner have the title examined. This process involves a search of the property records of the county in which the locus land exists. Most counties have surprisingly accurate records of who has owned the land for the last century, though in the majority of cases title examiners will go back an average of only sixty years.

Title examiners are searching for several things. Most important, they want to be certain not only that the present seller is in fact the present owner with a full legal right to dispose of the property but also that the present seller bought the property from someone who likewise had a right to sell it, and so on back through the years. Many times, there is present what is called a *defect* in the title. Someone in the past may have sold the property without having a complete legal right to do so, which means that the present owner does not have a perfect title.

Another common problem that turns up in a title exam is a mortgage once issued on the property that was not completely paid off or discharged. Although ordinarily this turns out to be a case of the discharge not being noted properly or *recorded* with the county authorities, the entire matter must be examined and rectified before the title will be deemed to be clear. Obligations that involve or that are secured by land continue to exist on the land and do not terminate with its sale or with the death of the owner who incurred that obligation. It is said that they *run with the land.*

If two owners before the present owner held a bank mortgage on the land that was never discharged by the bank, the mortgage would be assumed to be still outstanding and would in effect be an obligation on the present owner for as long as he owned the property. Once a cloud is located on a title, however, no bank attorney or buyer's attorney would allow his client to obligate himself to such an unsafe property. There is no sense in buying a $50,000 home if there is already a $20,000 mortgage outstanding on it from a previous purchaser.

In such a case, the bank attorney will try to contact the creditor who had secured his debt with the land and ask him to provide an official document stating that the debt was discharged. If the money is still owing, the balance would have to be cleared up before a new title would pass. This process sometimes requires contacting owners from years past or their surviving relatives. If the problem still is not cleared up, there are other resorts with the land court, but they are expensive and time-consuming procedures (such as land registration).

Title examiners search for other things that might "run with the land." An *easement*, a privilege or right granted to someone else to use the land, may also be a part of the story of the property. You would want to know if the Holy Name Junior High School, located behind your new home, possessed an easement allowing its students to cross your front lawn during school hours. Such an easement would likely show up either on a deed or on a separate written agreement between the parties who made it, although it can be created merely by operation of law or by continuous and open use.

If a previous owner owed money to a creditor such as the gas company or if he had a judgment entered against him in a court of law, there may be a *lien* or attachment on the property for the value of the sum owed. The lien is an obligation on the property that secures some debt or obligates some performance of an act, the satisfaction of which will satisfy the lien and allow its discharge. If a creditor has a lien on the property, he has the right to have it sold or otherwise applied in satisfaction of a debt.

Back taxes, tax waivers on deceased owners, information on whether the property was taken over by the city and then resold at an auction (often considered an inferior title), and other probate problems are some of the other things for which the title examiner checks. In most cases, the title will be found to be clear—or, with some legwork, clearable—and the title examiner lets the bank attorney know this through a long abstract or written history of the particular parcel of property.

Getting the Papers Ready

Once your bank attorney is possessed of a clear history of the property, he will then proceed to draw up the papers to the property. Under ordinary circumstances, it is the responsibility of the seller to produce a new deed to the house that lists the new purchaser and seller. The seller will have to hire a lawyer to draw this new deed, or he may engage the bank's attorney, who will already have all the information at his side.

Prior to the actual passing of papers the buyer by law must be furnished a form that will supply information about settlement costs. It will inform the buyer of the fees due the bank attorney, the costs involved in recording the change of ownership, the gross amount of money due the seller, any reduction in the amount due the seller, and the like. This form, called the Disclosure Statement, is issued by the U. S. Department of Housing and Urban Development.

Years ago, people would be present at their real estate

closings and would sit dumbfounded in total confusion while fast-talking attorneys divided up tens of thousands of their dollars. Now, the government requires the lending institution to issue borrowers with this advance disclosure to provide them ahead of time with a precise estimate of how their money is to be handled and disbursed.

The borrower is also entitled at the closing to a statement of actual costs paid; a form virtually identical to the advance disclosure statement, it gives a complete summary of the transaction as it has occurred.

Many attorneys, through oversight or neglect, fail to provide the borrower with the advance disclosure and final settlement statements. You as the borrower and consumer should insist on your absolute right to obtain a copy of each, in order that you can fully understand the disbursements and charges tendered with your own money. The Truth-in-Lending Act of Congress entitles you to this information before the passing, and it is inadvisable to attend the closing without it.

The bank attorney will prepare the mortgage and the *mortgage note*, which in effect conveys the property to the bank until the mortgage is paid off. It does not, of course, mean that the borrower or mortgagor is giving up his possession of the property. It is more of a lien against the property that can be foreclosed upon by the lender bank or mortgagee if the borrower does not keep up on his mortgage payments or otherwise keep the property in good repair.

THE CLOSING

After all the paperwork has been completed, the bank attorney will contact you as to the date for the passing of papers, often called the *closing*. The seller will often be present to collect his share of the money, though as long as he has presented the attorney with a signed deed conveying the property to the buyers in the proper manner, his presence is not required. It is certainly advisable, however, that he be in attendance in case of any dispute.

Prorated adjustments on items already paid for by the seller whose benefits the new owner will at least partially enjoy are usually made at the closing. For example, if taxes are paid on a calendar year basis and the seller has paid the taxes for the full year, he is entitled to a credit from the buyer for that portion of the year's taxes that represent the ownership by the buyer. If the passing is on July 1, the buyer owes the seller exactly one half of the taxes for the full year paid by the seller.

Similar adjustments are made for heating oil in the tank as of the date of the closing, water, sewer, or utility charges owing or prepaid, and so on. Such adjustments often involve negotiations, and the seller should preferably have an attorney present who is completely familiar with negotiating at closings.

At the passing, the new buyer will be required to produce proof of an insurance policy, usually in the abbreviated form of a binder, to prove to the bank's attorney that the home is insured up to its full market value, thereby furnishing the bank with security for its investment. It is always required by the lender bank that the borrower maintain adequate insurance on the property.

Once all the figures have been worked out and the necessary papers signed, the money is exchanged, mostly in certified or cashier's checks in an amount which the buyers have learned from the bank's attorney, usually the day before. The deed and mortgage will then be noted or recorded in the county office responsible for the registering and keeping of the deeds, usually called a Registry of Deeds. Once the deed is accepted by them, ownership of the home officially "passes" to the buyer or grantee. The passing is complete.

As the new owner, you should immediately notify the

local water and tax assessment offices of the change in ownership. This will not only insure a prompt updating of official records but also insure that the proper parties accurately receive the correct bills and will save them from the headaches of tracing lost bills, overcoming penalty clauses, and correcting irrelevant names on what should be your new bills. If it's winter and you're not moving in, be sure the heat is left on.

Do You Need Your Own Attorney at the Closing?

Many people try to save money by representing themselves at the passing. The new buyer, who is already paying the bank attorney several hundred dollars or more to process his mortgage, particularly attempts to avoid the added expense of another lawyer.

Having your own lawyer at the passing is money well spent. The bank lawyer's first loyalty is to the bank, which he constantly represents and which pays him handsomely for what is usually routine and financially rewarding work.

The buyer must pay for the bank attorney's legal fee, which means that if the buyer wants to be completely safe by hiring his own attorney, he will be paying two attorneys. Although this may seem like an overly cautious luxury, the enormity of the investment requires maximum protection. Your own lawyer can watch out for your interests and argue disputed points and adjustments with a loyalty solely to you. The bank lawyer is working for the bank, and his primary interest is in completing the mortgage paperwork with accuracy and care. Each lawyer performs a different function, and it is wisest to hire your own attorney to protect you in case of a conflict. The additional cost often proves to be a sound investment.

The seller, too, has too much at stake not to be represented. The private attorney's fees to the seller are not usually very high, often amounting to from one-half to one percent of the total purchase price, and his services may pay for themselves should adjustments be disputed or some other procedure weigh against the seller.

TIPS TO REMEMBER

After you have purchased your house, your awareness of the tips presented in this chapter may make the difference between having the house of your dreams or a house of nightmares. Your occupancy will be much happier if you move in knowing that you did everything as efficiently and inexpensively as possible.

- Hire your own attorney as soon as you are ready to sign a binder.
- The purchase and sale agreement can "make or break" a conveyance.
- Shop for a mortgage—not just for the rate, but for all the terms of the mortgage.
- If it's not in writing, it's not a part of the agreement.

4

Insurance

Insurance companies are nice folks to deal with, until it's time for them to pay a claim. A person who has paid his premiums promptly and then one day files for a legitimate claim may discover later that the company has ripped open a tiny loophole through which it hopes to escape any liability. Or, equally as common, a person may file a claim only to discover that under the conditions of the policy not carefully considered, the insurance company is under no obligation to honor the claim.

For example, a man who learns he has cancer may try to collect on his disability policy and be stopped by the insurer, who claims that because the cancer had probably been growing for years, it is an illness existing in the body of the insured before he took out the policy and hence is not a compensatable illness. Likewise, a policyholder may have decided that the time has come to have extensive dental work done, and believing that he was covered, obligated himself for thousands of dollars of tooth care. However, upon submitting his bills to his insurance company, he is horrified to find out that, although the company does pay for dental work, they only do so when a dentist or oral surgeon is required as a result of an accident or related illness.

Incidents like this are common; and whether it is a matter of interpretation or of locating that exception in the policy, you, as the policyholder, could find yourself in an awkward position. Some members of the insurance industry operate under the assumption that they owe the money to the insured, but why pay it willingly without the good fight? By circumvention and confusion, the insured person may actually be convinced that he does not qualify for money that is rightfully his. Even if he thinks he's entitled to it, the odds are fair that the insured will not know enough or be aggressive enough to fight the battle himself. Even if the insured consults with a lawyer and the lawyer sues, the odds are good that the lawyer will settle the case out of court for less than the maximum limits of the policy. Should the case go to trial, the insurance company may confuse the facts and consequently the jury enough either to win or to have an award ordered that is less than the full policy limits.

If the insurance company fails at all these steps, the most it will have to pay is the amount it would have originally had to pay if it had honored the policy in the first place. It has lost nothing. That cancer victim probably didn't have the time or the money to hire an attorney, while the insurance company is specifically geared with its staff of retained lawyers and investigators for such battles—part of what keeps insurance one of the must lucrative industries in the world.

Of course, things were not intended to turn out this way. Historically, members of a particular craft or trade would each contribute a sum of money to a common fund, to be used when disaster struck one of its members. Early insurance was thus a kind of mutual protection, where many people contributed a sum of money periodically, called a *premium*. The aggregation of this money would form a guaranteed payment to any contributor who suffered a loss covered by that fund.

INSURANCE TODAY

Insurance today is not much different. In an insurance contract, both parties agree in writing to undertake certain obligations. One party, known as the *insurer*, contracts to indemnify or provide compensation (in the form of money) for damage or loss to the other party, known as the *insured*. Certain causes for the loss may be excluded from coverage under the contract, but at least in theory these exclusions must be specifically mentioned in the contract.

The insurance industry, then, forms a network through which the losses of a limited number of people are divided among a large group of people, the latter group comprising the vast majority who do not make any claims in a given year but who pay premiums that are used to indemnify the losses of those who are insured and do claim that insurance protection.

In today's progressive world, where each person and each parcel of property faces imminent potential damage, there is insurance for almost everything. There is life insurance, automobile insurance, health insurance, disability insurance, marine insurance, even income insurance. Insurance remits to a designated party, known as the *beneficiary*, the amount of a proven loss incurred by the insured. This loss can be for loss of property, loss of life, loss of livelihood, or indemnification for a judgment against the insured, as in an automobile tort—as long as that loss is covered by the terms of the policy.

Because an insurance contract involves indemnifying someone for his losses, the insurance company will monetarily compensate for any loss incurred that is covered by the policy. The insurance contract, however, must be based upon some interest or right of the insured party that is affected by the loss. You could not take out property insurance on the White House, as you have no *insurable interest* in it, either at the time the hypothetical damage occurred or when the policy was purchased. If there is no insurable interest, there is neither the right to insurance nor any allowable recovery for damage.

You may take out a life insurance policy on the life of your spouse, because an insurable interest exists in that relationship. The same is true for a business partner. But you would not be able to take out a policy on the life of the Queen of England or the rock group *Queen*, unless some relationship involving an insurable interest existed between the parties when the policy was issued.

Of course, the individual who wishes to enter into a contract for insurance must be legally capable of making a contract.

The insurance company will not pay for losses ordinarily covered under its contract or *policy* with the insured if the insured has not kept his premium payments up to date. As in all contracts, consideration must be present. The regular payments remitted to the insurer, for which the insurer agrees to take on its obligations and issue a binding policy, constitute that consideration. If the insured stops making payments on those premiums, then he is withdrawing his consideration and breaching his end of the contract.

If a payment is missed, the policy will be said to have *lapsed*, and the obligations of the insurer will cease. Many people fail to realize this; when they fall short of cash they ignore the nasty notices from their insurance company and postpone making payments when due. When an unexpected loss occurs, they find the insurance company denying indemnification on the grounds that the policy had lapsed. It is a difficult position to overcome, particularly as most policies allow a company to declare the policy lapsed after the premium has been overdue for a specified period.

Insurance companies also avoid paying for losses ordinarily recoverable under the conditions of the policy when the insured has misstated or misrepresented information on his application for insurance. It may have been a false listing of his age, an incorrect description of the automobile to be covered, or the concealment of a recent illness. Because the insurance company bases its decision of whether or not to insure the applicant on the information provided on the insurance application, it can deny any responsibility for honoring that policy on the grounds of misrepresentation or concealment of a material fact.

This issue of representation is the hub from which many lawsuits radiate. Some people innocently fib about their age, which is a material fact in the matter of life or health insurance. Other people claim their automobile is garaged in a location other than where the car is housed in order to get a lower premium rate. Whatever the misrepresentation, the insurance applicant should be cognizant that all his subsequent premium payments may be for nothing if the misrepresentation is alleged and proven by the insurer. The insurer can rightly claim that the risk is greater than it was originally aware of when the insured applied for coverage and that it would not have extended that coverage had it known the full truth.

Most insurance policies contain a clause stating that the company will forego or waive its rights to deny coverage due to misrepresentation after the passage of a certain number of years. In other words, any defense the company might have against a claim will go by the boards after a given length of time; and it will have to aware benefits to the claimant irrespective of the misrepresentation. This waiver does not usually apply to fraudulent statements willfully made by the applicant, but it does cover the innocent factual misstatements to which many people are prone.

Whether misrepresentation is fraudulent or innocent or whether the applicant for the insurance had any intent to misstate the facts, the policy will be voidable. In order for concealment to effectively render a policy unenforceable, however, the company must prove a fraudulent intent was behind the concealment.

The People You Deal With
The insurance company insures or promises to reimburse the insured for his losses. The causes of damage for which the policy provides coverage are also called *risks*. The policy assumes the risks for covering a certain subject, be it the life of a person or the house or the merchandise in the store or whatever else the policy covers.

Insurance companies are regulated by the state in which they conduct their business. Most major insurance companies do business throughout the United States. These companies must be allowed by the various state regulatory agencies to operate within the boundaries of that state. If they do not obtain that permission, any contracts they enter into in such states are unenforceable. Violations, unfair treatment, delayed payment of benefits, and other consumer complaints are most effective when initially made directly to the state regulatory insurance commissions. Companies who had been unwilling to act prior to a complaint to an insurance commission have been known to do an overnight turnabout when faced with the possibility of economic sanctions therefrom.

Insurance agents are employed by the insurance company. As agents, they fully represent the company they serve, and commitments entered into by them bind the principal company as would the acts of any agent. They not only deal with applicants for insurance, but with individual brokers as well.

These insurance brokers are different from agents in that the broker does not represent the insurance company as its authorized agent. In fact, brokers are small business people who act independently of any one insurance company. They generally have their own clientele for whom they act as agent. They place the insurance applications of their clients with any one of several companies, and they are responsible for securing for their clients a sound policy with a registered and sound insurance company.

Although brokers are not agents in actuality, they function from a legal viewpoint as agents and may be held liable for any negligent acts or improper dealings regarding the brokers' representation of an insurance company to a client. Like the companies themselves, brokers are licensed and regulated by the state. If a consumer is dissatisfied with his broker's handling of his insurance, a complaint to an insurance commission often goes a long way.

THE INSURANCE BINDER

It takes about a week or two before an insurance company can approve an application for insurance. However, most people need coverage immediately. To effectuate this, the agent for the insurance company issues to the applicant what is called a *binder*, a temporary policy that covers the applicant against loss until the full policy is approved.

Unless the agent has been given authority to issue a binder, a binder will be invalid. If the binder is validly issued, it is effective only until such time as the company acts upon the application. If the application is accepted, the insured owes no additional money for the time covered by the binder. If the application is refused, then the applicant may owe the insurer a minimal premium only for the few days the binder was in effect.

Under no circumstances does the issuance of a binder obligate the company to issue a regular policy to the applicant. However, if a loss does occur after the acceptance of the binder but prior to the issuance of a policy, the insurance company would still be required to indemnify the loss, as long as the agent was authorized to issue the binder.

Binders are generally not effective until the application is accepted in matters of personal health or life insurance, and the reason should be obvious. Until a physician has examined the applicant, the insurer would have no rational basis for ascertaining the nature of the risk in accepting the applicant. Whether he has a heart condition or leukemia or is perfectly healthy would be relevant and material to the ultimate decision of the company to insure or not insure.

LIFE INSURANCE

In consideration of a periodic premium payable to the insurance company, the life insurer pays an agreed sum to a named beneficiary of the insured upon his death. Beyond this, the types of insurance policies available vary greatly according to the number of premium payments, when the policy will expire, and other such conditions.

Perhaps the most common type of life insurance is the *whole life policy*, for which a set premium is paid each year during the entire lifetime of the insured. Upon the death of the insured, his named beneficiary is paid whatever was the full face value of the policy. Every year the insured pays the same premium on a whole life policy, although he may turn it in at any time during his life for whatever is the cash surrender value at the time; this prorated value is usually listed in a table that is a part of the printed policy.

The *face value* of any life insurance policy is, as its name suggests, the amount actually specified on the face of the policy, the total collectable when you die. As long as the policyholder has paid his premiums faithfully, his beneficiary is entitled to that face value, whether he has been making payments for twelve years or twelve months.

A *term policy* requires that premiums be paid annually for a specified period of years. Most term policies run between five and ten years. The amount of each premium payment remains constant throughout the term period and is based upon the age of the insured. However, if the insured wishes the policy to continue in effect upon the expiration of the term, he must renew the policy, usually at an increased rate dependent on his increased age. If the insured dies during the term, the insurer will pay the full face value. Because in this type of insurance there is generally no cash surrender value provision and coverage is for a limited term, premium rates tend to be lower for term insurance.

Other types of policies are written for certain periods of time, but their coverage continues for the life of the insured. For example, under a *twenty-payment policy*, the premium is paid in twenty installments. No additional premium payments are required, and the coverage extends until the insured dies, at which time the insurer pays over to the beneficiary the face value of the policy. Thirty-payment policies operate on exactly the same principal, except that because the premium payments stretch out over a longer period, each one is smaller and thus more affordable for individuals with more limited resources.

The insurer in an *endowment policy* does not necessarily pay the named beneficiary upon the death of the insured. Rather, these endowment policies award the full amount of their face value at the conclusion of the terms specified in the policy. Thus, if the insured has an endowment policy written for twenty years and is living at the end of that term, the policy is terminated and he is paid the full amount. At his option, he may continue the policy with the insurer or take out a different type of policy. If, however, he dies during the term, the insurer will pay the full face value of the policy to the named beneficiary.

Endowment policies have the advantage of giving a large lump sum to the insured—if he survives the term—at a time in life when such an award may be most needed. If he doesn't survive the term, then his named beneficiary will still receive the full face value upon his death. The premiums are constant and, as in most life insurance policies, are based upon the age of the insured at the time he applied for the policy. Buying this type of insurance at an early age can thus be a tremendous money-saving investment.

An individual may also reach an agreement with an insurance company whereby he will pay the company a specific lump sum or single large payment in exchange for the company at some later date paying him back a set sum of money periodically for the remainder of his life or for a stated term of years. This type of arrangement is called an *annuity*.

Each of these policies has different features, different strengths, and different drawbacks. The individual who shops for insurance must be careful to weigh each and as best as possible determine how much insurance protection he will need and how much protection he feels his named beneficiary will need. He must also be wary of certain insurance salesmen (most notably cousins and friends of the family) whose personal gain is increased as the cost of the policy is increased. No policy should be entered into without a complete understanding of the cost and benefits therefrom and a realistic appraisal of how much might be too much.

The Beneficiary

It is of primary importance to grasp the fact that once a beneficiary, the person named to benefit from the proceeds of the policy, is listed in a life insurance policy, he is deemed by the law to have a property interest in the proceeds of the policy. As such, the insured cannot change the beneficiary at his own desire or whims unless he has previously reserved the right to change the beneficiary and has written that agreement into the policy. The beneficiary is considered otherwise to have a right to the proceeds upon the death of the insured.

If a husband names his wife as a beneficiary the wife would remain as the beneficiary even after a divorce unless the husband had been possessed of the foresight to reserve the right to change the beneficiary.

The majority of modern policies today reserve this right in advance for the insured. However, it behooves each applicant for life insurance to be certain that the policy includes a statement granting him this right unequivocally.

The named beneficiary in a life insurance policy has the right to the proceeds from the policy even if the insured left all his property in his will to someone else. Life insurance proceeds are deemed to be outside the estate of the deceased and separate from his other property.

As the policyholder, you have the right to name any person or any thing as your beneficiary. Your favorite charity, your lover, or your pet (collectively or separately) can be legally named by you; restrictions of family or marriage cannot be imposed. And, unlike the named beneficiary of a will, an embittered relative cannot contest the life insurance policy demanding that he be awarded a portion of the insurance money by virtue of his relationship to the deceased.

HEALTH AND ACCIDENT POLICIES

Many of the cautions given in the previous section on life insurance are likewise applicable to the many health and accident policies today. Health policies differ in many respects from one another. The provisions in their incontestability clauses, the exclusions of chronic illnesses, coverages for accidental injury or death, or coverages for dental work vary between policies and can mean the difference between coverage or exclusion when a crucial illness arises.

Additionally, different policies vary as to the coverage provided for hospitalization, visits to the doctor's office, and pharmaceutical charges. Worth investigating as well is the coverage (or lack thereof) a particular company provides for debilitating illnesses that are due to mental rather than physical causes. Some states have provided through legislation that psychological counseling allowances must be a part of all health policies.

As an illustration of the variances in coverages, consider this case: The presence of pylonidal cysts is an extremely common condition today, particularly among white-collar workers. This is a chronic condition that often does not seriously impair the victim for several years, only to flare up unexpectedly. Some policies would exclude this condition from coverage because it is chronic, and all such illnesses are not covered under some less satisfactory policies. Others will exclude such conditions for a short period of time, to be certain that the insured has not taken out the policy just to have his chronic condition operated on. After this limited time, the condition will be covered. Blue Cross usually requires a six-month waiting period for treatment, whether for calcium on the knee, arthritis, or that pylonidal cyst.

As mentioned previously, you must have an insurable interest in the life of a person before you can take out a policy, be it life or health, on that person. Parents can take out life insurance policies on their children; but Marc's parents cannot take out similar insurance on Jennifer, Marc's favorite playmate.

There are also several "pre-paid" health plans in operation throughout the United States. Examples are the Harvard Plan in Massachusetts and the Kaiser Plan operative in several states, including Ohio and California. Under these plans, the insured pays a set premium and is thereafter covered for nearly all his health care needs, whatever the seriousness of the illness, its duration, or the amount of hospital care required. Pre-paid service will often include eye and dental care as well as provisions for regular check-ups. Pre-paid care has a vested interest in preventive medicine.

Some pre-paid services have their own hospital, medical

staff, and facilities; others have a cooperative arrangement with the existing medical establishment. As some people object to being forced into accepting care at one named institution and prefer a choice, a careful study of the benefits and requirements of each health plan should be made before finally selecting one for you and your family.

Prior to taking out a policy for health insurance, you should check to see what type of plan might be offered at a group rate either where you work or at some organization of which you are a member. Asking will do no harm, and nowadays most employers and organizations have made at least some provisions for health care, sometimes unbeknownst to those for whom such a plan has been implemented.

FIRE INSURANCE

Normally when an applicant seeks to purchase fire insurance, the company issues to him a *binder* pending delivery of the actual policy. If the applicant suffers any loss during the time the binder is in effect, such loss is fully recoverable. The binder remains in effect until either the company gives notice to the applicant that it refuses to cover him or the company issues the permanent policy. Written notice is required of a refusal or cancellation by the company to the applicant.

Most states have adopted, for the sake of clarity, the same form of fire insurance policy. The terms and conditions in the contracts for fire insurance are thus uniform. Each policy states a face amount, which is the maximum liability of the insurer in the event of a loss. In turn, upon delivery of the permanent policy, the insured is responsible for paying all premiums when due.

Fire insurance policies not only cover property damaged by a fire but also protect against damage incurred from smoke and water used in connection with any fire on the insured premises. In order to be compensable, however, the damage must have been directly caused by the fire. Thus, water-soaked or stained property resulting from the fire would be deemed to be "fire losses."

There are many considerations that must be kept in mind, for your insurance agent will be very precise about them if you ever find yourself in a position of having to file a claim. First, a fire must literally be a fire; the most basic dictionary will tell you that means it must be visible, in an active stage of combustion, and must have light and heat. Second, in order to receive compensation, the fire must be out of control and it must be a hostile fire. Lastly, the fire itself must be the direct cause of any damage; if the fire was a secondary reaction you will have difficulty recovering, inasmuch as the fire was caused by another element and that other element was what triggered the ultimate damage.

If your child is playing with a chemistry set in the attic and accidently allows chemicals to leak into the boxes where you have stored your winter clothes, the resultant burning is by definition not a fire, because it does not have a glow and luminosity about it. That "fire," even though it may eat through the clothes and continue on through the floorboards, is merely the process of oxidation at work. Chances are, your policy does not cover you for that particular damage.

Suppose you owed an extremely rare cookbook that you had gone to the extreme of listing separately in your policy under household goods. One evening, as you were consulting this book in preparation for dinner, the telephone rings. Inadvertently, you place the book on top of the stove, not realizing that a burner is on. When you return from your telephone call, you discover to your horror that your book is in flames and completely destroyed. You will not be able to collect because the fire that destroyed the book was not a hostile fire.

The concept of a fire as a direct cause of damage probably is the one aspect that will affect most people's lives, and therefore is a crucial one to understand. If you light a cigarette and put that cigarette out in a kerosene can, the explosion that results will most certainly burn your house down, but it was the explosion that caused the fire. The fire was a secondary reaction. The heat of the cigarette could not have caused a fire capable of burning your house down, and therefore fire was not the direct cause of the damage. Fire is the final outcome of many an instance where chain reactions are involved, but the destructive flame and heat of the fire must be present first and must not have been caused by anything else, if your insurance company is to be held liable.

In the application for insurance, it is incumbent upon the applicant to list a complete and accurate description of the property to be covered by the policy. A correct description in the application, later repeated in the policy, is mandatory; without it, the insurer will not extend coverage and will not be liable for damages to unreported property or merchandise. Similarly, any property moved from a described place will not be covered under the policy unless that change is reported. The insurer can only be required to insure that property of which it has full knowledge and can assess its risk in covering. Therefore, if you decide to move that expensive piano from your living room to the garage for the summer, it's worth a call to your agent.

You should also be aware that there are certain items you might keep in your home that an insurance company will not be liable for under any circumstances. Such things as currency, bills, notes, deeds, and securities should be kept elsewhere, for if they go up in smoke with the rest of your possessions, you cannot recover.

As in other forms of insurance, fraud, concealment, or a misrepresentation of facts will render the fire insurance policy void. For example, applicants often have within their knowledge an additional hazard to the property (stored kerosene, for example) on the location to be insured. Such hazards or increased risks that are unreported will relieve the company of any responsibility therefor.

The exact amount one should carry on his home and its furnishings is an individual choice. Once again, it is as wasteful to overinsure as it is to underinsure. The amount of insurance purchased should depend primarily upon the value of the home and furnishings to be insured, in other words, on their replacement value. Consultation with a broker is the most sensible approach when determining policy limits, but caution is advisable, given the special interests of the broker.

It may be recommended that *extended coverage* be included in a policy for damage due to wind, civil disturbance, explosion, smoke, or war. The regular fire policy, which excludes such losses, specifically includes the above-cited perils at an increased premium. Certain specific types of explosions or accidents are even excluded from extended coverage, and thus a close reading of the separate extended-coverage policy is urged.

If a loss is suffered by the insured, he must notify the insurer, whether the agent or a broker, without delay. It is his responsibility to give the insurer a complete listing of the damage to the property and the goods therein, together with the amount of money he is claiming was lost as a result. If he does not promptly comply with this procedure, the company may deny any liability on the claim.

Either party may cancel the policy of the insured. If the insured party cancels, his cancellation will become effective as soon as the notice of cancellation is received by the insurance company. Alternately, if the insurer cancels the policy, its cancellation usually does not take effect until five days after the insured receives notice from the company. This delay is designed to allow him the opportunity to secure other insurance, so that he will not suddenly be left unprotected from the moment of notice of cancellation.

AUTOMOBILE INSURANCE

Once again, the rule of thumb in this type of insurance is: understand before you buy. Most people do not understand the fundamental nature of insurance and usually spend far more money than is necessary.

Insurance is naturally going to be costly. Roughly one third of every dollar is absorbed into insurer expenses. Only the remaining two thirds can thus be returned to the consumer over the long haul. Because auto insurance is so costly and is really meant to protect against significant losses, the shrewd buyer will purchase coverage only for potentially large losses.

Many states make it compulsory to carry a minimum of insurance covering bodily injury to others where the injury is caused by the auto of the insured. The insurance company will pay only if its insured or someone else using his car with his consent is legally responsible for the accident. If someone with this type of coverage is using an auto he or she does not own at the time of the accident, the owner's auto insurance pays up to its limits before the driver's company will pay up to its limits.

Differing states have varying minimum requirements for bodily injury or property damage coverage. You should check into the cost of increasing your coverage in these areas beyond the minimum. With hospital and repair costs skyrocketing, the minimum often is not enough, and doubling your existing coverage may mean a difference of only a few dollars. Likewise, check into options such as insurance against uninsured motorists or for passengers in your vehicle, which can often be obtained for very minimal prices.

Collision insurance pays for any direct or accidental damage to your auto caused by a collision. If your automobile is over five years old, the cost of carrying collision insurance may exceed its value to you. For example, if your present car is worth $1000 wholesale and your policy has a deductible (the minimum amount you must pay before the insurer will begin to pay) of $200, the maximum the company will pay for your car if it is totalled in a wreck will be about $600. They will pay you what the car is worth wholesale, less certain deductions and adjustments. Thus, if you forego collision coverage that might cost $300 per year, and have no accidents for two years, you have saved in premiums in those two years the entire book value of your car. If you have no accident for three years, you effectively have made $300 if in the third year your car is totalled and you chose not to carry collision protection.

Collision insurance is not the only auto insurance you may want to do without. Comprehensive insurance pays for direct and accidental damage or loss to your auto other than damage caused by a collision. Vandalism, fire, theft, and certain disasters are covered under comprehensive insurance. However, particularly in urban areas, comprehensive coverage can run into several hundred dollars.

Given the value of your car, it may be far more economical to get a locking steering-wheel brace and gamble that your car will not be stolen. If after two years your car is stolen, you still may come out ahead by having saved nearly the full value of the car in unspent comprehensive premium payments. If you feel you must have comprehensive or collision insurance, buy them with a sizeable deductible. Companies offer discounts of up to thirty-five percent for taking a $500 deductible policy. No deductible means the company will be paying for all the damage, and the premium charges will be accordingly high.

If your state has competitive rating, where different companies charge different rates, shop around. Price is important, but it shouldn't be the sole consideration. The quality of service you are offered from the insurer or from the agent is also a part of your purchase. Seek out the best combination of price and good service for your individual requirements. See what your insurance will cost if you stay with your present insurer, and then try other insurers for comparison.

Mutual companies occasionally pay dividends to their policyholders at the end of the year, which should also be considered. Above all, good driving will mean lower premiums, because the more the company has to pay out, the more you will pay. Many states have now adopted merit rating, where every accident you cause can raise your rates, said surcharges being based only on fault. These surcharges are then returned, with interest, to drivers with good records. The greater the pool of bad driver surcharges, the less costly insurance will be to good drivers. It is an idea of merit that serves as both encouragement and incentive for good driving and lower rates.

TIPS TO REMEMBER

The two most important factors to be considered when purchasing insurance are: (1) Be sure you have the proper insurance for your particular needs; too much is as wasteful as too little. (2) Be sure you read your policy carefully and that you understand completely what you are and are not covered for. If you don't understand a portion of the policy have someone who is an expert in reading detailed, legal clauses decipher it for you. Do not rely on your insurance agent to be your sole source of interpretation. And naturally, if you do not like what your potential policy has to offer, don't take it.

In summary, you should be aware of the following items and questions relative to any insurance policies you might already have, or that you are considering:

- What damage, illness, or accident will your policy *not* cover?
- Do you have the option to change your beneficiary, if you should so desire?

- Do you have the type of life insurance that will best suit your needs?
- Are there any group health plans available to you?
- Do you need extended coverage for your personal property?
- Is your automobile liability insurance ample to cover any serious accident you might be involved in?
- Don't be railroaded, either into obligating yourself to a policy or into accepting a settlement that is below what you feel you are entitled to!

5

Wills and Trusts

Perhaps the best way to understand the purposes of a will is first to examine the word itself. A person's "will" is the expression of his desires. If you have a "will" to do something, you are consciously and deliberately making a choice; and thereafter you will be making an attempt to implement that choice.

A *will* in the law is an instrument that declares the choices of a person about the disposition after his death of all those matters including land (*real property*) and personal property over which he had control during his lifetime. It authorizes another person, known as the *executor* (or executrix, if that other person is a woman), to implement those choices on behalf of the person who has died (the *decedent*).

The executor is bound to act in accordance with the wishes of the decedent as expressed in the will. The court in turn operates to insure that the executor is faithfully and honestly executing his duties and that all those who are to receive benefits from the possessions and property (the *estate*) of the decedent do in fact receive what the decedent intended for them. Those who potentially will receive such benefits are called the *beneficiaries* of the will.

Too many otherwise prudent people choose not to make known their last wishes formally through the instrument known as a will. As a result, the court will still have to appoint an executor who is known as an *administrator* (or administratrix, if a woman). The administrator will divide up the estate usually among the closest surviving blood relatives and the surviving spouse, if there is one. This division might often not be the choice of the decedent, but by failing to draw a will he has forfeited his right of choice. The final disposition of the property of a decedent who dies *intestate*, without a will, may not be consonant with his wishes, but may rather be the end product of feuding relatives, court personnel unknown to or disliked by the decedent, and imposed state laws.

The naming of an executor is not the only privilege forfeited by those who do not make a will. The will can otherwise make known the wishes of the decedent in such important areas as who will assume the responsibility of raising surviving minor children, burial plans, the establishment of trust funds, and the complete disposition of all personal property and real estate over which the decedent had control during his lifetime.

In addition, a will is of important use in saving taxes on the estate of the decedent. Income taxes, property taxes, estate taxes, and other potentially applicable state and Federal taxes all come into effect upon the death of every state and United States resident. Proper planning through the creation of wills and related trusts can result in enormous tax savings not only for the decedent's estate but subsequently for his surviving heirs as well.

REQUIREMENTS OF A WILL

For a will to be valid it must satisfy certain requirements of law. First of all, a will in most states must be in writing. Oral dispositions of property are not usually honored by the courts, and it is easy to see why: Any one of several people who knew the decedent could potentially claim to have been promised the decedent's mansion, and how could it conclusively be decided which of the various selfish claimants was telling the truth?

Certain states do allow oral (or *nuncupative*) wills, but generally they are permitted only for very limited purposes. Those jurisdictions recognizing oral wills limit their validity to the disposition of a small amount of personal property, generally under a few thousand dollars. There is a further general requirement that witnesses to the oral will either reduce the will to a subsequent writing or otherwise testify before an appropriate judge as to the express words of the decedent. No state allows for the disposition of real estate by an oral will.

Returning to the standard written will, the document must then be signed by the maker of that instrument. Without the valid signature of the maker of the will, there can be no will. By his signature, the maker is showing to the world that the will represents his wishes and the action is of his free will at the time of signing.

The signature of the maker must be witnessed by two or three witnesses, depending upon each state's laws. The witnesses are not witnessing the contents of the will, and they do not even have to see any of the will. They are only witnessing the signature of the maker and the state of mind at the time of the signing.

While any person with the capacity to contract can be a witness to a will, if you have even the remotest suspicion that you might receive anything under the will, *do not act as a witness.* Because you are what is termed an "interested witness," your signature as a witness would be invalid and could jeopardize the validity of the entire will. Worse still, whatever was left to you in the will will be denied to you and passed instead to the blood relatives of the decedent as if he had died without leaving any will at all (*intestate*). A will that is in the handwriting of the *testator* (the person leaving the will) and not properly witnessed or signed—often called a *holographic will*—is invalid in most states. California will allow such a will, provided it is in the testator's penmanship and is signed and dated by the testator at the end of the will.

One of the most common errors perpetrated in the execution of a will is where spouses innocently sign as witnesses to each others will, as often spouses will execute their wills in their lawyer's office at the same time. The rule that interested parties to a will should not act as witnesses is equally applicable to spouses. *Do not* sign the will of your own husband or wife.

Other Requirements

The maker of a will must further have some property that can be passed or transferred to a named person or *legatee*. (The named person to whom real estate or real property is left is called a *devisee*.) If a will bequeaths (gives) nothing, there would be no point in honoring that will.

The maker of a will must also have the legal *capacity* or power to form a contract. He must, for example, be of minimum age to qualify as an adult (usually between eighteen and twenty-one, depending on the individual state). He cannot be drunk or insane or under undue influence or fraud, for then he would neither be acting of his own free will nor possessed of a genuine capacity to contract.

The court insures through its supervision and system of checks that the last will of the decedent is carried out with full fairness and accuracy in accordance with his stated wishes. The will has an effect as though the decedent who left the will, the testator, were alive, and the words in the will are his binding orders that the court is charged with enforcing. As long as the will was drawn according to state laws and procedures and was of the free will of the maker, it will be held to be valid and enforceable by the courts.

The Will as Final Expression

The courts will not normally allow for the express wishes of the testator to be contradicted. Even if it is proved that the testator grew to hate his best friend subsequent to his leaving that friend all his property under his will, the court will not overturn his will. The will is deemed to be the final testament of the testator's wishes; he always had the option to alter it during his lifetime if he had so desired. Were the court to allow changes in a will on alleged alterations in personal feelings, precious few wills would ever be honored and all the court's time would be wasted on picayune arguments between greedy contestants. Of course, if there was undue fraud or influence in the making of the will, the court will hear evidence to substantiate that allegation. Anyone who attempts to contradict or contest the will has the burden of proving that the particular section of the will or in fact the entire will is invalid. It is otherwise presumed by the court that the will is valid and that when signing it the testator knew it was the valid expression of his final wishes.

For example, if Sam Senile is being cared for by Nurse Greedy, and as a result of her flattering him with false paeans to his looks and sex appeal he leaves her everything in his will, such a will will probably be upheld by the court as valid. Even if the aggrieved contestants could show that the nurse was cajoling Sam to get his money, the court would not contradict Sam's written word on how he wanted to leave things. The usual presumption is that he was of sound mind and in the exercise of his free will at the time he made the will. Flattery would not be enough to cause a will to be disallowed or declared invalid.

Competence of Testator

There are generally three classes of people who would be *competent* (possessing the required legal qualifications) to testify as to this "mental state of the testator" at the time he made his will. The testator's family doctor, who presumably knew of the state of health of the decedent, can swear to his sanity around the time of the making of the will. Experts in the field of the treatment and analysis of mental disorders are also allowed to testify as to the condition of the decedent. Finally, the witnesses to the will, who were present at the signing of the will and who could best judge the condition of the testator at that time, are deemed to be competent to render their opinions as to the testator's sanity.

It would have no bearing whatsoever on the validity of the will that the decedent was totally insane for six years before his death. The only state that is relevant is the state of mind of the testator *at the time he drew the will*. Thus, even if the testator were partially mentally unstable, as long as he drew the will during a lucid interval observed by witnesses, he will likely be judged competent and of sound mind for this purpose in the eyes of the court. The fact that he was merely peculiar or eccentric does not conclusively prove unsoundness of mind. If it did, many wills would have to be disallowed.

Fraud and Undue Influence

Returning to our greedy nurse, let us suppose that Nurse Greedy told Sam that unless he willed all his property to her she would pull the intravenous needle from his arm or refuse to administer his medicine. That clearly would be undue influence, and evidence of such conduct as the motivating factor for his bequest to Nurse Greedy would certainly be admissable as evidence to overcome the presumption of free will. Undue influence forces the testator to act against his will despite his knowledge of the actual state of circumstances. If Nurse Greedy married Sam in his sickbed and kept from him the fact that she was currently married, only to insure his leaving everything to her, then that will could be successfully challenged on the grounds of fraud, which involves acts to intentionally deceive the testator of the true circumstances while ostensibly allowing him to act freely. Note the distinction between mere flattery, as in the earlier example cited in the previous section, and this type of blatant illegality.

CHANGING THE WILL

The relevant rule of thumb to follow is that, once you draw a will, be certain it is kept up to date. If you become estranged from one of your children, you have the absolute right to re-draw your will and intentionally omit that estranged child. If at one time you left your former lover some valuables in your will and since then you have grown to hate each other, any evidence of the recent hatred will probably be irrelevant if you die, because you knowingly left your will as it was and your heirs are bound by the last will of your written word. It is assumed that had you wanted to omit this ex-friend from your will, you would have taken steps to do so. Certainly, the courts are not about to psychoanalyze each relationship remembered in a will to see what the possible subliminal implications might be in each. They must assume out of practicality that the last will and testament of John Jonesberg was precisely that: his last will.

Codicils

The most common means employed to change, update, or otherwise alter a will is by the creation of a *codicil*. A codicil is an instrument signed by the testator subsequent to his making the original will. It refers back to the original will and amends a part of that will.

The codicil does not invalidate the original will; it alters it. The new terms expressed in the codicil replace the outdated terms in the will that are specifically referred to in the codicil. The basic document thus stays in existence as the valid wishes of the testator, and the codicil or codicils exist with it as effective amendments thereto. Upon the death of the testator, they are all offered for probate as his last will and testament.

To be legally effective, the codicil must be executed with the same formalities required of the will itself. It must be signed by the maker, witnessed by the requisite number of people, and be of the free will and sound mind of the maker. In fact, a properly executed codicil can validate an improperly executed will. If, for example, the will was not signed by the proper number of witnesses but a subsequent codicil referring to that will was signed properly, then the codicil may make both the will and the codicil effective.

Many people erroneously believe that they have legally changed their wills by crossing out certain phrases and inserting substitutions in their places. Corrections done directly on an existing will are not valid, although such alterations will not destroy the will entirely. The will may still be established and proven according to its original wording, but the corrections or interlineations will be discarded. Alterations made prior to the signing and witnessing (the *execution*) of the will will be valid, provided they are initialed by the maker or otherwise referred to before his formal signature.

As a will never takes effect until the death of its maker, each person retains the power to cancel or *revoke* his will at any time and for any or no reason. This is most commonly done in one of two ways. Firstly, a person may revoke his will by drawing up another will or codicil. The subsequent will usually contains a clause that specifically states that it supercedes and revokes any prior existing wills. Such a revocation by a subsequent instrument may also be implied from the new will even though it is not specifically stated. Its inconsistency with the prior existing will operates as an implied revocation.

It should be noted that if the two instruments are only partially inconsistent, the later will or codicil will supercede and control only to the extent that the two documents are inconsistent. If the earlier will has been only partially superceded, both may be admitted to probate, although the latter will is given priority wherever ambiguities exist. Because this situation can become both confusing and crucial, the safest course to follow when having a new will drawn is to be certain it expressly revokes all prior wills.

The alternative method of revocation is physically to destroy the old will or codicil. This can be done by tearing it, burning it, or the employment of any other imaginable method of destruction. All copies of old wills should also be destroyed. Although there is a presumption that if the original will cannot be found it was revoked, often copies of wills have been admitted to probate through the sometimes erroneous court finding that the will was accidentally lost but should be honored as if still existing. This is unlikely, but it does happen; it cannot happen if all copies of a revoked will are completely destroyed.

Effects of Marriage on a Will

Unfortunately, many people leave their last will and testament as it was written years before. Some marry, unaware that, in most cases, marriage revokes any prior existing wills. The reason for this rule of law is that the courts assume that once a party marries, the entire scope and emphasis of life changes and that the party now has a new primary source of personal and tangible devotion. This new relationship was not foreseeable at the time the old will was drawn, and thus the courts conclude that the will could not realistically be viewed as the valid wishes of the party who made the will before entering into the marital relationship. Only if the will states that it was being drawn in contemplation of an impending marriage will it be upheld after the marriage.

The result of this rule is that many people who think

they are protected by a will are treated upon their death as though they died *intestate*, or without a will. In other words, if the will is invalid, it will not be allowed as the last will and testament of the decedent, who will, in effect, be deemed to have died without leaving any prior enforceable wishes.

Effects of Divorce on a Will

Although marriage usually revokes a will, divorce may not. Diane Divorcee may have been tickled pink to get rid of Paul Playperson, but the will she made years before on their honeymoon that left everything to her beloved Paul upon her death may be found to be valid. The logic here is that merely because a party divorces her spouse does not mean she wishes to leave him nothing. There are deep bonds of love that continue between people long after the legal bonds of matrimony are severed. The courts cannot accurately assume that an adversary relationship is the natural product of a divorce. Personal devotion and ties of time, family, and mutual experience can continue to unite a divorced couple. Therefore, immediately upon divorce, it is best to re-examine your will to be certain you wish to keep things as they are or, where appropriate, make a new will reflective of your changed circumstances. Otherwise, a detested ex-spouse may be the beneficiary of your estate.

ADMISSION OF THE WILL TO PROBATE

As discussed at the beginning of this chapter, an *executor* is that person authorized in the will by the maker of the will who will be responsible for carrying out the conditions expressed in the will. He has been chosen by the maker usually because he is trusted. Unless he is exempted by the testator, he may nonetheless be required to post a bond. A bond is a kind of insurance that acts to protect all the potential heirs against any selfish or unethical conduct on the part of the executor as he carries out his dispositive duties.

The official appointment of the executor named by the testator is approved or allowed by the court after the will has been accepted by the court as the valid final testament of the decedent. This acceptance of the will is termed an "admission of the will to probate," because the proper court for such an action generally is called the *Probate Court*. Historically, the term probate related to the actual proof of a will. Proof was offered before a duly authorized person—often called a *surrogate*—who determined the validity or invalidity of the instrument. In England, this Probate Court was established in 1857. Today in the United States, the Probate or Surrogate's Court has *jurisdiction* (power) to completely supervise and manage all matters relating to the settlement of estates of decedents. Probate courts are usually located in every county. Once it appoints the executor, the court keeps a close watch on the executor, who ultimately must account for every penny that was left by the testator. At the end of a year's time, he must further show how everything was distributed in precise accordance with the directions in the will.

The executor's affirmative duties include the collection of debts, the payment of outstanding bills, the adjustment of claims, the distribution of the assets of the estate as per the provisions in the will, and the filing of all the accounts, tax forms and waivers, and inventories required before the estate of the decedent will be deemed cleared and closed.

The executor need not be a lawyer or a mathematical wizard. Most of the time, the surviving spouse or next of kin is named as executor of a will. As the complex legal work must be done by a lawyer anyway, there is usually nothing for the executor to handle beyond his abilities. A lawyer may, of course, be named in the will as executor; and this step is often advisable and can simplify the proceedings, particularly where close relatives are either nonexistent or hostile.

Also, the testator can request that a bank be named executor; one of its officers will act as executor when the proper time comes.

Executors take title to personal property but not to real estate that passes to the heirs or devisees. However, where it is the duty of the executor to settle the debts and legacies of the estate, he may for this purpose sell real estate by obtaining special permission from the court through a license to sell real estate.

Appointment of an Administrator

The alternative to not naming an executor in a will or to not having a will at all is for the court to appoint a person to perform the function of the executor upon the death of the decedent who died intestate. The person the court appoints to administer the affairs of the intestate estate is called the *administrator*. He can be any person interested in the estate of the deceased, a creditor of the deceased, or any suitable person. Generally, the surviving spouse is first granted the right to be administrator, followed by the next of kin and the creditors.

An administrator must usually post a bond, which as mentioned is an instrument that obligates him to faithfully discharge his duties or pay a certain sum of money to cover the costs of his failure of performance. Bonds may be obtained through an insurance company, or private parties may in effect guarantee performance of the administrator by placing their property with the court as security or surety for the administrator. The reason for this is that if the decedent's estate is worth $5,000 in cash, what otherwise would prevent the administrator from skipping town with the money—or distributing it according to his individual whim? Particularly where the court does not know the individual and the administrator was not chosen by the decedent, this personal insurance against misconduct is a safeguard against selfishness or partiality on the part of the appointed administrator.

Cost of a Bond Versus Cost of a Will. Most state courts require a bond from executors and administrators at least equal in amount to the value of the estate of the decedent. This can be a very expensive procedure if the administrator must obtain the bond through an insurance company or bonding agency. These outfits usually keep a percentage of the bond as their profit. But if you name an executor in your will, you can exempt him from furnishing that bond. In effect, you're telling the court that you trust your executor to do an honest job; lacking any contradictory evidence, the Court will approve the named executor without a bond. A will can thus pay for itself within a month, because whatever you spent for the will is saved by the exemption of the executor from posting a bond. If for no other reasons than to pick your own executor and save money in the process, every person really ought to draw a will.

CONTENTS AND OMISSIONS

A will can be half a page or one hundred pages, depending on the directions of the testator, the size and value of the estate, and the complexities of the various gifts or legacies, called *bequests*. The articles or clauses of a will cover a wide variety of subjects. Provisions can be included, for example, to establish the source for the payment of death taxes, debts, charitable pledges, funeral expenses and arrangements, existing mortgages, and the costs of administration.

Disposition of Personal Property

The testator may dispose of all his personal effects and other tangible personal property through clauses in his will. Although it is common practice simply to leave all one's personal property to a loved one, many people want to leave specific items to individual beneficiaries. This is permissible and often leaves people deeply touched by the thoughtfulness. However, it more often leaves people bitter and feeling cheated. It is far wiser to choose the few people who mean the most to you and to bequeath significant gifts to them. The people you omit will still be bitter, but no more so than had they been left a little.

The practice of leaving somebody a dollar is also unwise and unnecessarily time-consuming. Reminders of ill feeling after death serve little purpose except to spite, and the old saying of laughing last can come back to haunt the testator's survivors.

Anyone who is left something in a will generally must provide his assent to an accounting of the proper distribution of the assets in the estate; the unwillingness of an heir angered by a small bequest to provide that assent often means that a circuitous, time-consuming, and expensive procedure will be required before the allowance of the final accounting of the estate. Also, as a named heir, such a slighted person still has standing to object to certain other procedures and in general can choose to make life miserable for the executor and survivors of the testator. It is thus advisable either to leave someone nothing or a significant share.

It is unwise to leave someone something (a *bequest*) as a joke out of some frivolous whim. The beneficiary of a humorous corkscrew may nonetheless be treated as a named beneficiary in the will, with the standing to object to the will or otherwise inhibit the final probating of the will.

Children Omitted from a Will

Many people are under the erroneous assumption that the best way to disinherit an heir (usually a spouse or a child) is to omit him from any mention whatsoever in the will. Unfortunately, the result of such a total omission can often be antithetical to the intent of the testator. Called *pretermitted heirs*, such heirs who are omitted without mention can in most states contest the will on the grounds that they were inadvertently forgotten by the testator. In many states, part of this situation is addressed in what are called the *Omitted Children's*

Statutes, whereby omitted children take the same share of their parents' estate that they would have taken had the parent died intestate or without a will. In short, an omitted child has a claim against the estate, if the omission does not appear to be intentional.

Thus, Pop's will may provide that his sons Abraham and Isaac should share in his entire estate equally. When Pop dies, he dies leaving three sons. The third son, Jacob—as a natural heir—could claim the share he would have taken had Pop died intestate; this would amount to one third, as the estate would have been divided equally between the three sons had Pop died with no will. (A discussion of the division of property among next-of-kin where no will was left follows later in this chapter.)

The situation would be completely different, however, if Pop had his lawyer draw a clause that said, "I specifically omit my third son Jacob from my will, and this omission is intentional." Jacob then could not claim accidental omission and would have no grounds upon which to contest the will. In that case, Abraham and Isaac would each get one half, and Jacob would be shut out.

The important thing to remember here is that if you are a parent and want to leave out one of your children, do so intentionally and specifically in the will; if you are the child of a recently deceased parent who has left a will, check the will to see if your name is mentioned, because even if it's not, you may still be entitled to a proportional share of the estate.

Rights of Surviving Spouse

In addition to the provision discussed earlier that allows an unmentioned spouse who married the testator after he has made a will to petition the court to have the will disallowed, there are other protections allowed spouses omitted from the wills of their deceased spouses.

The major protection is the statutory provision in most states that gives the surviving spouse the absolute right to a designated share of all the property in the late spouse's estate. In effect, this is a restriction on the testator's rights, as under no circumstances can the surviving spouse's rights of inheritance be totally defeated.

Within a certain prescribed period of time after the will has been presented for allowance, the surviving spouse can contest or *waive* the provisions of the will by filing an objection in the court where the will was offered for allowance. This right is, however, personal to that surviving spouse only and cannot be passed on to other relatives. In fact, this right to waive the will is automatically terminated upon the death of the surviving spouse. The notable exception to this rule is where the surviving spouse has deserted the deceased spouse or chosen to live apart from her.

A surviving spouse only sparsely provided for in the will may elect either to accept the share specified in the will or to waive the will and accept the statutorily designated share of the net estate of the testator irrespective of the will. Prior to exercising this option, a lawyer should be consulted; but you should know that the right exists.

Some states, such as California, protect the rights of the surviving spouse through the system of community property. In these states, each spouse is treated as having a half-ownership in most property accumulated during the marriage. Thus, each spouse has only the right to bequeath one half of that property, because the surviving spouse already owns the other half. Because of the recognition in such states of the immediate possessory interest of both spouses, the rights to waive or contest the will as just discussed would be, of course, inapplicable.

TRUSTS IN A WILL

Many wills contain what we call *trust provisions*. A trust is created when the owner of money or property surrenders or bequeaths legal title and control of that property to another person or institution known as a *trustee*. This surrender or bequest is implemented for the benefit of a third party (often several third parties) known as the beneficiary.

The trustee is "trusted" to manage the property for the benefit of the beneficiary or beneficiaries, as directed by the maker of the trust (the *settlor*) in the trust instrument or the will itself. If the trustee acts recklessly or in his own selfish interests, he is in violation of his trusted or *fiduciary* duty and may be held personally responsible for his indiscretions.

Some trustees are given greater latitude in the management of whatever is contained in the trust than others, depending on the conditions set forth by the settlor. For example, some trustees are given the power to sell the real estate in the trust. Others are not allowed to touch the contents or *corpus* of the trust until the named beneficiary reaches a certain age, at which time the trustee's only duty is to release the corpus to him.

Inter-Vivos Trusts

Some trusts are created by people during their lifetime and are not a part of their wills. These *inter-vivos trusts* are drawn for a variety of reasons, one of the most common being to take a piece of property out of the name of the real owner, thereby potentially immunizing that property against certain types of restrictions that might otherwise be imposed on it as a result of litigation against the owner.

For example, if Larry Lawsuit owns a home in his name, and a judgment is rendered against him for $20,000 by a court of law, that house may ultimately end up as a kind of security for that money. If he does not come up with the cash, he may ultimately be forced to liquidate his assets, namely the house. But if Larry had placed the house in a realty trust created ostensibly for the benefit of his five-year-old niece and named his mother as trustee, it would no longer be a personal asset of his and probably would be unreachable by his creditors. The deed to the house would be in the name of the trust, even though he had created the trust and still lived in the house.

Inter-vivos trusts relating to property must be in writing, and the settlor cannot be the beneficiary as well. Furthermore, the property cannot be sold until the expiration of the trust, as provided for in the trust agreement or by operation of law. Several restrictions, some of them not mentioned here because of their complexity, operate in a trust situation; it is still a useful legal creation of which you should be aware. A lawyer should be consulted before any action is taken on a trust, as an improperly drawn trust can cause far more disadvantages than benefits. But a properly executed inter-vivos trust can bring untold advantages to the settlor as well as the named beneficiaries.

Using Trusts

Trusts are most typically employed in wills to provide for named beneficiaries who could potentially be minors at the time of the death of the testator and hence incapable of receiving a bequest of devise outright. Certainly, it would make little sense to leave a six-year-old ten thousand dollars. Leaving it directly to the parents of the minor child might result in the parents using the money for their own benefit. The correct method effectively employed is to leave the money to the parents, but in *trust* for the benefit of the minor child. The parents then become responsible as trustees to control the corpus according to the dictates of the trust agreement. The money is left in their control, but it ultimately must be accounted for to the benefit of the beneficiaries.

Thus, Uncle can leave Mom and Pop $10,000 in trust for Niece Patty, with certain attached conditions: The principal $10,000 should be released to Patty when she reaches the age of 21; the trustees can invest the money in savings banks only; and they may use the interest on that principal sum at their discretion and at any time, as long as it is for the health or education of Niece Patty. Uncle has thus prevented the money from being squandered or used in any unauthorized manner other than that he intended and has insured that when Niece Patty reaches age 21, she will have the full amount of the principal. Additionally, he has given the parents the option to use the interest in their discretion only under sensible conditions.

Marital Deduction Trusts

There is also a device known as the *marital deduction trust*, allowed under the provisions of the 1954 Internal Revenue Code. It makes it possible for a married person to leave up to one half of her or his *adjusted gross estate* (the total worth of everything over which the decedent had control and ownership less certain deductions) to a surviving spouse in a certain prescribed manner. If written properly and according to precise regulations, the result can mean that half the estate will be exempt from the federal estate tax otherwise due from the estate of the decedent.

Marital deduction trusts are very complicated, and a lawyer must be consulted not only to draw one but to advise you whether it is even appropriate. In the majority of situations of Mr. and Mrs. Average American, few advantages would be gained by the use of the marital deduction. Particularly if your net worth approaches six figures, however, you ought to be aware of this potential tax break that may or may not exist as a part of your will.

INTESTACY

As defined previously, those who die without leaving a valid will or whose will has failed are deemed to have died intestate. Each state has designed its own laws of intestacy to regulate the succession of property. While these rules result in inheritances that probably do not correspond with the true intentions of the decedent, he and his heirs must pay that price for his failure to make proper provisions for his death.

You will remember that an administrator must be appointed by the court to perform the functions of an executor. Generally, the nearest relative to the decedent entitled to share in the estate will be appointed, provided he is both willing and competent. Most often, this is the surviving spouse. If there is no spouse, the appointment will be granted to the person who qualifies for the larger share of the estate, be it a child, a parent, or whichever relative is first in line as next of blood kin.

Most states give the surviving spouse everything in the estate of the decedent if there are no other surviving close relatives. If there are children that survive with the spouse, then the spouse will receive either a third or a half of the estate, and the children will equally divide the balance among them. If any of the children has predeceased the decedent, then the children of that deceased child will share equally in the amount to which the deceased child would have been entitled.

Some states place a limitation on the amount the surviving spouse can receive where there are no surviving children but there are other surviving relatives. Others give the surviving spouse everything. Where there is no spouse and no close relatives, complex charts on descent and distribution show who is the relative closest in the blood line to qualify for the full inheritance. (Stories abound of second cousins once removed who one day find themselves the happy subject of a million-dollar inheritance, though it is unlikely to happen to any of us.)

The important point to remember is that there is in every state an orderly line of inheritance that provides for the fair and impartial distribution of all the assets of a decedent who dies without a will. These laws vary on such diverse issues as the rights of adoptive and so-called illegitimate children, the percentage various relatives can inherit, and like topics. But whether or not a will was left, the estate of every deceased person (with the rare exception of a pauper) must be probated.

SHOULD YOU MAKE A WILL?

The cost of a will varies according to the complexity and labor involved in its preparation. It also depends largely upon the attorney you use. Whether the will employs trusts, the number of named beneficiaries, and clauses particularly tailored to your specific needs are some of the items that can mean a will of greater expense.

The simple will, typified by the husband leaving the wife everything and providing that if she dies first then everything is to be divided equally among his surviving children, can be as inexpensive as fifty to one hundred dollars. If any of those children is a minor, then a trust would have to be written in at a slightly higher cost. Executing a codicil can be less. As with any service, prices vary greatly.

The important thing to bear in mind is the freedom you buy for yourself at a relatively minimal cost. You will have planned as carefully for what occurs after your death as you had cautiously provided all during your lifetime. Your loved ones, your children, and your possessions will be disposed of in the manner you direct by a person or institution in whom you have placed your thoughtful trust.

The alternative is to die intestate and let the laws of intestate succession and confused (and occasionally garrulous) relatives decide what is best for them to do with all you have built during your lifetime. On balance, it doesn't seem a valid alternative. If you don't have a will, make inquiries of at least two attorneys. If your will exists, check it. It is at once the easiest and most dangerous task to set aside until a convenient time that, without immediate persistence, too often never comes.

II

OTHER LEGAL TOPICS

6

The Law of Torts

WHAT IS A TORT?

A *tort* is a civil wrong that causes either a physical or an emotional injury. The victim of that injury may sue the person who inflicted it and can receive compensation for suffering the resulting harm.

We use the word "civil" to mean "as between persons." This is a difference between torts and crimes. When someone commits a crime he is both prosecuted and, if found guilty, punished by the state according to its statutory laws. The wrong that he has committed is not only against his victim but also against the populace as a whole. Crimes are committed against society, and the state is the named plaintiff for whom the actual victim offers testimony to prove the charges.

On the other hand, a tort lawsuit is personal between the

one who committed the tort and his victim. The purpose behind the civil lawsuit is to return the victim to the same position he was in before the tortious offense was committed. This is usually accomplished by the victim receiving a sum of money from the person who committed that tort.

The main difference between tort law and criminal law is the goal each is intended to accomplish. Criminal law is the law of prevention, punishment, and rehabilitation, whereas tort law is the law of compensation.

Torts are *wrongs*. By this it is not meant that torts are merely unethical or immoral acts. Rather, they are acts that injure personal interests deemed worthy of compensation. Moral ideas of right and wrong, while relevant to the evaluation of tort case law, do not control it.

INTENTIONAL TORTS

There are two groups or classifications of torts: intentional torts and negligent torts. Simply stated, *intentional torts* are those civil wrongs committed by someone who is substantially certain that injury will result from his action. The actor (or person who has committed the tort) need not have any hostility or malicious reasons for committing his act. His motives or purposes may be pure, and he may even think that his act served the best interests of all concerned. But if the act is one which we could say is likely or foreseeable to produce an injury, then the law concludes that the actor has the intent to commit the tort.

A person who explodes a bomb in a taxi may intend to kill only the passenger. Yet as it is reasonable to infer that the taxi driver may be injured or killed by the explosion, the law concludes that the bomber in fact intended to injure the driver. The same legal conclusion is reached if the actor mistakenly struck at the wrong taxi.

The idea of intent is related to the idea of predictability.

Thus, when the law says that the bomber intended to injure the driver it means that the resulting injury can be predicted from his action. Let us now consider intentional torts in detail.

Battery

As we have previously mentioned, criminal law protects our interest in remaining free from bodily injury caused by another. In fact, the law of torts goes much farther. The interest protected is not only freedom from physical damage to our bodies, but also protection against body contact or touching of an offensive or rude nature. The degree of force may be irrelevant. Spitting in someone's face, while not causing severe harm, is a battery. Simply stated, a *battery* is an unpermitted, unprivileged, offensive contact with the body of another or with something closely associated with the body by an act intended to result in such contact. Let us examine this more closely.

An unpermitted touching is one to which the person touched does not give his consent. A running back playing in the NFL consents to being touched by the other players during the game. The rules of football permit one player to knock down another during the course of a play. A defensive player's skill is based in large part on how well he can do this. That same running back does not consent to a disgruntled fan tackling him when he leaves the locker room after the game.

Society has certain customs that may be called "socially acceptable touchings." To live our everyday lives, we consent to these types of physical contact. Otherwise, we could not live peacefully side-by-side with other people. It is neither pleasant nor comfortable to ride in a rush-hour New York City subway in mid-August. Commuters are packed into the trains and frequently jostled about. The touchings that occur on these rides only aggravate a bad situation; they are offensive. But the necessity of getting to work relatively inexpensively makes it impractical and intolerable for commuters to sue for battery each time they are touched on the subway. Those suits would cause more injury than they would cure. Living in the America of the 1970s requires that we all by implication consent to some contact. Whether it is offensive depends not on the victim's quirks but on whether the average person would be offended.

An unprivileged touching is one that is committed by a person who has no legal right to touch the victim. A police officer making a valid arrest presents an example of a privileged touching. In the course of their duties policemen often arrest unruly and violent individuals. The person being arrested undoubtedly does not consent to the physical contact that may be visited on him. The law gives policemen this right to touch such an individual irrespective of the manner that can be offensive to the individual. This type of nonexcessive, unconsented-to touching is permitted in order that the police may perform their important job.

The physical contact required for a battery is not limited to a touching of the victim's person. It may include more than just physical contact with his arms, legs, and face. Any article or item connected to the victim that is offensively touched gives rise to a battery. Even though a purse snatcher grabs only a woman's purse and never places his hands on her person or clothes, he commits a battery against her. The purse is considered to be part of her body.

Whether a battery has been committed in the vast majority of instances involving physical contact depends primarily on whether the victim can answer yes or no to these questions: (1) Was the contact offensive? (2) Did the victim consent to the touching? Generally, an unconsented to and offensive touching is a battery.

Assault
The tort of *assault* is often mistaken for the tort of battery. Battery involves freedom from an offensive touching. As-

sault involves freedom from the awareness of an impending battery. No touching is necessary, only the impending threat of a battery coupled with some act toward accomplishing that battery.

Throwing a punch and hitting someone is a battery. Throwing a punch and missing is an assault. The injury to the victim is not physical but mental. It is the awareness that a battery is about to be committed.

Awareness is not the same as fear. A weakling can assault the toughest fighter, even though the fighter is not afraid, merely by making the fighter aware that a battery will occur.

The assailant must have an apparent and present ability to carry out the battery for an assault to exist. The word apparent is used to show that an assault may occur even when the assailant does not in fact have the ability to commit a battery. The victim only has to reasonably believe that a battery is about to be committed against him. One who lunges at another with what looks to be a knife commits an assault even if he has no intention to stab the victim or if the knife is actually rubber. As long as the victim was reasonable in his awareness that he was about to be stabbed, an assault occurred.

The victim must also reasonably believe that the battery is impending. No assault is committed when the alleged assailant is too far away from the victim to harm him. Nor does an assault occur when the alleged assailant merely prepares to take some action, as when he shows a weapon such as a blackjack. By the same token, words alone are not an assault, no matter how threatening. It has been generally thought that words do not produce an awareness of an impending touching.

An assault is committed, however, when violent words are accompanied by an act which, without the words, would be inoffensive. For example, in a heated verbal exchange between two known enemies, one raises his arm to scratch his head. The combination of words and gesture may create a reasonable awareness of a forthcoming battery which in other circumstances may be unjustified.

False Imprisonment

The law of torts protects our interest of freedom of movement or locomotion. An actor cannot intentionally confine another within boundaries.

The injury to the victim in *false imprisonment* is his awareness that he is confined. A person must have the power to move, and false imprisonment occurs when he is prevented from exercising that power.

The boundaries within which the victim is confined may be physical surroundings such as a room, a house, or a ship. The means of confinement may be of words or conduct which threatens harm to the victim if he does not stay put.

Restricting or preventing the victim from using important property may be a means of confinement. For example, if the actor takes the victim's car keys to stop him from driving, false imprisonment may occur. The boundary of confinement is the distance the victim wishes to travel away from his car. As one may not be able to abandon a car, the victim in effect is forced to remain close.

Moral pressure is not enough for false imprisonment. Physical force or its threat is required.

One is not falsely imprisoned if he has a reasonable means of escape. When a victim must risk injury to escape, the means are not reasonable. If one door is blocked from the victim's use, it may or may not be false imprisonment, depending on whether or not there were alternate doors and windows available for the victim's safe egress.

Trespass to Land

Trespass to land occurs when someone intentionally and wrongfully enters land possessed by another. The trespasser does not have to know that the land he entered is possessed by another. He may actually, but mistakenly, believe that he owns the land. As long as he intended in fact to enter another's land, he is a trespasser.

A person enters land wrongfully when he has no right to enter. Among those who have a right to enter land are owners, lessees, licensees, possessors of legal authority (such as a federal marshal informing someone a lawsuit has started against him), and rescuers.

No real property damage is required for trespass. The trespasser need not destroy land by bulldozer or some similar means. The injury to the possessor is the mere entry itself.

When a true possessor of land discovers that someone has entered his land, he will probably sue not to collect monetary compensation, but rather to protect his right to the land. He wants a court to say that, as between him and the trespasser, he has the right to undisturbed and peaceful enjoyment of the land. This is an excellent means for the landowner to protect his substantial investment.

The ways in which trespassers can enter land are varied. Entry may be accomplished by someone wrongfully walking on the land, someone rightfully on the land but then refusing to leave when the right to stay has ended. For example, when student protesters enter a college administration building during its operating hours they may have a right to be there. After the building closes, however, the students are at that point probably trespassers because their right to remain ends. And even where a protester causes a sympathizer who otherwise would not enter the building to enter by falsely assuring that the entry is permissible, that sympathizer himself becomes a trespasser, in addition to the protester.

A trespasser is responsible and must pay compensation for any injury his entry causes. The trespasser's liability does not depend on his being at fault. For example, a balloonist once landed in a garden and was held liable for damage caused by a crowd which rushed in, on the theory that he prompted their intrusion.

Trespass to Chattel

A *chattel* is personal property, as distinguished from real estate. Chattels are infinite in number. They include such items as livestock, jewelry, appliances, cars, and books. A person commits trespass to chattel by causing a chattel of another to become reduced in value, quality, or condition.

As in trespass to land, trespass to chattel is a tort against possession. The actor cannot escape liability by saying that the true owner must bring the lawsuit. For example, one who is loaned a brand new bicycle may sue the actor who intentionally bends the handlebars. He does not have to wait for the real owner to sue.

Unlike trespass to land, however. trespass to chattel requires actual damage to the chattel. Someone wrongfully sitting on another's car may not be sued for trespass to chattel. Actual damage sufficient for a trespass to chattel claim would require, for instance, that the actor had broken one of the car's headlights.

Conversion

The rots of trespass to chattel and *conversion* are often confused with each other. Both involve action against the possession of a chattel. Trespass to chattel impairs the item in some way, whereas conversion is the intentional and wrongful control over another's chattel. In the case of conversion, the converter must pay fair market value for the chattel, not merely damages. As title to the goods passes to the converter after payment, this is actually a forced sale.

A thief is a converter, but a converter is not always a thief. One who innocently buys a stolen chattel from a thief is a converter. In some states the chattel's true possessor must make a demand to the innocent buyer before he can retake the goods. In other states, he need not.

An important question is: How much control over chattel is enough control to be conversion? The answer depends on factors such as the actor's intention, how long the goods are in the actor's possession, and whether the event is harmless. For example, if a customer leaves a restaurant with the wrong hat, walks a few steps, realizes his mistake, and returns the item, there is no conversion. On the other hand, there is conversion if he keeps the hat for eight months or if it is shown that he intended to steal the hat in the first place. The last two situations show a severe interference with the rightful possessor's hat and a clear-cut intent to exercise control over it.

Changing the location of another's chattel may or may not be conversion. Factors to be weighed are whether the actor notified the possessor of the change and whether the new location is convenient and accessible. Assume that one who has recently rented an apartment finds the previous occupant's chair, which the previous occupant refused to remove. The present occupant does not convert the chair by storing it at a warehouse provided that he tells the prior occupant of the storage, the warehouse is reasonably close in distance to the apartment, and the warehouse has regular business hours.

Conversion may occur when someone who has a right to possess a chattel refuses to give it back to one entitled to it. If, for example, a coat-check person intentionally delays returning a coat for ten minutes because he is not sure who the true owner is, there is no conversion. But if his intent is to retain the coat indefinitely, conversion takes place. In any event, the person entitled to the chattel must make a demand for the chattel before the possessor has to return it.

Intentional destruction of the whole chattel, even by one in rightful possession, is conversion. Incomplete destruction which drastically alters the chattel's character, such as cutting a skirt too short for the owner to wear, is also conversion.

A harmless use of the chattel by one in rightful possession will not be conversion. If a car owner parks his car in a friend's driveway with the understanding that the friend may use it for errands, there is no conversion when the friend drives it to go to a funeral. If the friend drives to a city hundreds of miles away for a weekend, conversion may be found.

Intentional Infliction of Mental Distress

The *intentional infliction of mental distress* is an act done or words communicated with the intent to cause aggravated mental distress and which cause such distress. The injury is inflicted to the victim's emotional stability, but some states require that physical injury to the victim must accompany the mental suffering.

Generally, insults and abusive language are not sufficient. The acts or words must be more offensive than ordinary street talk. If a person who is ordinarily thick-skinned would be distressed, the tort may be committed. However, employees on a train, bus, and other modes of transportation open to the public may be liable for words or acts that are less severe in offensiveness.

Conduct or words that offend the morals of any decent society are sufficient for the tort. These acts or words must be grossly outrageous. When a woman is emotionally distressed and physically injured because she is told as a practical joke that her husband was maimed in a car accident and is lying in the middle of the road, the tort is committed. Likewise, when the actor knows the victim is easily emotionally distressed at the sight of certain conduct or by hearing certain words, the tort is committed even if the act or words would not offend an ordinary person, provided the distress is severe.

PRIVILEGES

As a general rule, an actor will be liable and forced to pay compensation when he commits an intentional tort. This general rule has several exceptions, which are privileges the actor may assert. These *privileges* serve as defenses to any intentional tort that he otherwise may have committed. When he successfully asserts a privilege as a defense, the actor is not liable for any damage he caused the victim. The actor will not have to pay compensation. The privileges are discussed in the following.

Consent

The victim's consent to any act committed against him that may be a tort usually excuses the actor's liability. A victim consents to an act when he permits it to happen. There are two types of consent: express and implied.

Express consent may be given by an explicit statement granting permission. The statement may be oral or written. In a Sunday touch-football game, the participants will explicitly state that there may be blocking, but not below the knees.

A victim's conduct may show that he *impliedly consented* to the tort perpertrated against him. Silence may also be enough for implied consent. One who holds his arm out for a vaccination without protest impliedly consents to receiving the needle. The act of holding out the arm and the accompanying silence when the needle is administered relieve the vaccinator from any liability for battery.

The inner or secret feeling of the victim is irrelevant in determining whether he impliedly consents. In the example just described, even if the patient did not want to be vaccinated, the vaccinator would not be liable. The important factor is what outward manifestation, what conduct or appearance, the victim projected to the actor. If it is reasonable to believe that the victim's outward conduct expresses agreement to the act, there is no liability. It is reasonable to conclude that when a person extends his arm for vaccination, he consents to be vaccinated.

As we have seen, custom or social usage may imply consent. Remember the example in the discussion of battery regarding riding crowded New York subways. Social usage dictates that when we ride the subway we consent to some touching. We consent merely by remaining silent and boarding the train, knowing of the usual subway conditions. Each time a passenger enters a subway car, he does not announce to the other passengers that he consents to being bumped. Physical contact in a subway is a way of life. Our consent is taken for granted.

A person's consent only includes the act to which he gave consent. The actor may not exceed the consent given. One who consents to lending his car for a five-mile drive does not consent to a cross-country expedition.

A novel problem of consent involves the extent to which a paying spectator at a hockey or baseball game consents to being struck by a puck or ball. In hockey, pucks frequently fly over the protective glass surrounding the rink. One might conclude that the average spectator knows this and is therefore put on notice that he may be struck. But what if this is the spectator's first game and he had no knowledge? These are the gray areas of which lawsuits are made and argued.

In baseball, foul balls and home runs are hit into the stands constantly. It is part of the game for a fan to grab a souvenir. It is extremely difficult for a spectator to claim that he did not know this. But what if a relief pitcher, out of anger, intentionally throws the ball at a fan in the stands? Is it reasonable to conclude that the spectator impliedly consented to his silence to being struck by a baseball hurled at about 85 miles per hour at him? This does not seem to be one of the risks a person would be aware of even if he had attended a hundred games. Some courts claim that the whole problem may be solved when the spectator first buys his ticket, because each one generally contains a disclaimer of liability. On the other hand, does the spectator really consent to the mad tantrum of a childlike player warming up in the bullpen and not even in the game?

Of course, consent that is given because the person

granting consent was fraudulently misled as to the nature or character of the act consented to will negate that consent. If a patient is fraudulently told he has cancer when the doctor only wants to induce the patient to consent to an experimental treatment for his own research, the patient will later not be deemed to have consented to the treatment.

A patient's consent to his doctor's treatment presents special problems. Generally, a patient must consent to any operation or treatment. Two exceptions exist: (1) when the patient is unconscious or in an emergency and (2) during an operation if the doctor discovers a new condition endangering the patient's life or limb. Doctors do not have, however, a free license to perform surgery or treat patients at their whim.

Consent must be informed and intelligent. This means that a doctor must tell the patient the risks involved in any operation or treatment. The doctor does not have to disclose the risks if the patient is unconscious and in an emergency condition, or in a case when informing the patient of the risk is so detrimental that it will do more harm than good. Patients should be sure that they understand all risks involved and all the medical terms doctors use in describing their maladies and suggested treatments.

Depending on the state in which the victim wishes to sue, a person may or may not be permitted to consent to a criminal act. If one can consent to a criminal act, he will not be able to sue and receive compensation for injuries sustained during the commission of the crime. One who cannot consent will be able to sue and receive compensation. In many states a woman under a certain age may not legally consent to sexual intercourse. Even though she acquiesces in and encourages the act, her partner will not be permitted to use her consent as a defense to battery. (The same rule rendering minors incompetent of consent applies in criminal law as well; thus, even with consent, the actor may be charged with statutory rape if he has sexual relations with a minor.) Public policy requires that the law protect certain classes of people from their own poor judgment.

Self-Defense

In self-defense, a victim may use any reasonable force against another necessary to prevent personal injury that he has good cause to believe will occur. It does not matter that the victim was in fact wrong in his assessment of the severity of the danger. If the victim had sufficient reason to believe that he would be injured, he will not be held liable for using force. Factors such as the assailant's past conduct and reputation determine whether the victim was reasonable in using force.

A victim may *not* use excessive force on his assailant. He may use only enough force to protect himself, and generally he may not use greater force than was directed against him. If one is punched in the mouth, he may not shoot the assailant in response. If one shoots a trespasser and kills him, the trespasser becomes the victim, while the victim of the trespass may be criminally charged with murder or manslaughter and sued under tort law as well.

Once the danger has passed, the victim's right to use force ends. He may not exact retribution by injuring his assailant. Courts are the proper forum in which to vindicate one's interests if an injury has occurred and the immediate threat of danger has passed.

Ordinarily, a victim must make every possible effort to retreat from his attacker. When such efforts are futile, he may defend himself. A victim need not retreat from his home when attacked there. At least one state (Massachusetts) recently modified this rule and requires a victim to retreat from his home when he is going to resort to lethal force against his assailant.

Defense of Others

States differ in the protection they give one who uses force to defend another. Some states do not recognize this privilege at all; in them, one is not privileged to aid another. Others grant the privilege if the person defended had the right of self-defense. Should the defender assist the wrong party (the attacker) he is liable for injuries to his victim. Still other states grant the privilege only if the defender had reason to believe in the necessity of defending another. Should the defender assist the attacker in these states, he is not liable for injuries to the victim, a finding which encourages assistance to those in need.

Defense of Property

A person may use only that force which is reasonably necessary to protect his property. Generally, this is force not calculated to inflict serious bodily harm. Spring guns, for example, may not be used in defense of property as they are excessively dangerous and can result in greater harm to the offender than potentially could exist for the initial victim.

Recovery of Property

In limited circumstances, force may be used to recapture property wrongfully taken. The recapturer must act swiftly after his property is taken. Any undue delay in pursuing the actor ends his privilege. He must also make a demand for return of his property. Should the thief resist, the recapturer may use reasonable force to retake his property. Reasonable force is not force calculated to inflict serious bodily harm. If the belligerency escalates, the recapturer has the privilege of self-defense.

Storeowners lose millions of dollars each year to shoplifters and are placed in a precarious position. When they have reason to believe that a patron is stealing they must either permit the thief to walk away with the goods or prevent him from leaving the store. This latter course of action subjects them to charges of false imprisonment and slander (to be discussed later), even if they make an honest mistake.

Many states by statute now permit a storekeeper to detain and question anyone reasonably suspected of shoplifting. It should be noted that this is an extremely restricted privilege, limited only to the discovery of facts.

Detention must be for a short time only. In one instance, a thirty-minute detention in a restaurant for failure to pay the bill was judged unreasonable because the bill had been paid, and compensation was awarded to the victim. The person detained may not be arrested by the detainer, nor may the detainer use the detention to coerce or procure a confession.

Generally, a patron may be detained only if he is on the shopkeeper's premises. But some states permit detention if the patron is in the immediate vicinity of the premises. Unfortunately, these states do not precisely explain what geographic area encompasses the immediate vicinity of a store.

NEGLIGENCE

We are all familiar in a generic way with the term *negligence*. It is generally thought that when someone is negligent, he has acted carelessly and not prudently. The negligent actor has not done those things which an ordinary man of ordinary intelligence exercising ordinary judgment would do to prevent the injury. Technically, this is called the "reasonable man" standard.

A person in an emergency must act as a reasonable man who is in that particular emergency would act. Likewise, a person mentally or physically handicapped must act as a reasonable man possessing such a handicap would act. A minor, although liable for his torts, must act as carefully as would an ordinary person of the same age, experience, and maturity. But when a minor engages in an adult activity, such as driving a car, he must act as carefully as would an ordinary adult.

It has been said that "negligence does not exist in the

air." An actor can be negligent in his conduct towards another person only if he owes that person a duty to be careful.

Because every move that we make, every action that we take involves in varying degrees some risk to another, no duty towards another exists if the risk of harm is justified. We are justified in acting in a way that might harm another if an ordinary, reasonable man would act in this way.

There are three considerations which determine whether a risk incurred is justified or negligent: (1) Is the harm a foreseeable result from the act? (2) Should the harm occur, is it serious or mild? (3) How difficult is it to prevent the harm?

Assume for instance that a pedestrian in a densely populated area is struck by a car going 55 miles per hour. Applying the above-cited tests: (1) It is not at all unusual for a car travelling at 55 miles per hour in a location with many people to hit someone. Speeding cars hit pedestrians daily. (2) Certainly an injury sustained by one hit by a car is serious. (3) To prevent the accident, the driver only has to slow down to 20 or 30 miles per hour, which takes little effort. The risk the driver took that no one would suffer injury was not justified because the likelihood of harm was foreseeable, the gravity of harm was great, and the burden of preventing the harm was small. Thus, the driver owed a duty to the pedestrian to be careful and was negligent in causing the injury.

It should be noted that negligence may occur either because of an act or a failure to act. It is negligence for a homeowner not to remove from his front steps a skateboard that has been there for two weeks. However, one does not have a duty to incur a risk. Thus, a person is not negligent for refusing to save a person from drowning (although once he moves to save the victim, he assumes the duty to complete the effort within reason).

The relation between two people determines just how careful one must be towards the other. A possessor of land has a duty to a trespasser that is the same as his duty to a social guest, to refrain from wanton or reckless conduct. But his duty to a person on the land for business purposes is to refrain from acts of ordinary negligence. The land possessor in most states may be less careful in his dealings with trespassers and friends than he may with businessmen.

Generally, a landlord is not liable for injuries sustained by his tenants or their friends in the leased areas once the tenants have moved in. The landlord is liable for injuries caused by hidden dangers in the leased areas about which he did not tell the tenant. He is also liable for injuries sustained by tenants or their guests in the common areas if he is negligent. Common areas include stairs, hallways, laundry rooms, and the like.

For an actor to be negligent he must cause the victim's injury. To understand how an actor is liable for injury to another we must distinguish factual cause from legal cause. Factual cause means that if the actor had not done what he did, no injury would result. If a car driver did not drive 80 miles per hour in a 30-mile-per-hour zone, thirty minutes prior to an accident, he would not have arrived at a crosswalk in a manner and time to hit a pedestrian.

Legal cause is different. Legal cause means that the actor is liable for injuries to the victim only when (1) the harm that occurs is the kind of harm that might foreseeably result from the actor's conduct and (2) the victim was close enough to the actor in time and space so that the actor's conduct would foreseeably endanger the victim.

As an illustration, examine the situation where the driver exceeded the speed limit thirty minutes before his accident. The first criterion is satisfied. The kind of harm that occurs when a driver travels too fast is a car accident. But the second criterion is not satisfied. The actor's only conduct that could give rise to negligence occurred many miles and minutes away from the victim. To put it another way, the accident was too remote from the negligent act to hold the actor liable. Thus, even though an actor might in fact cause an injury, he might not *legally cause* the injury. If there is no legal cause of injury, the actor is not liable.

Even though the actor's conduct towards the victim is negligent, there are circumstances in which the actor will not be liable for injury. They are:

Contributory Negligence

If the victim's conduct was itself negligent in that it did not protect him from the actor's negligence when it could have, the actor is not liable in most states. Thus, a man who stands in the middle of the dark road at night directing cars away from his disabled car may be found to be *contributorily negligent* when hit by an oncoming car. His conduct is careless enough to have contributed to his own harm.

Assumption of the Risk

A person who knows the nature of a risk and voluntarily incurs it may not recover from that injury. A person aware that stairs are not safe who ascends them anyway relieves the owner of the stairs from liability, even if the owner is negligent in maintaining the stairs in that condition.

MISREPRESENTATION

Consider the following situation. John Smith buys a used car from a local dealer. The dealer orally assures John that the car has travelled only 5,000 miles. As proof he shows the car's odometer, which reads 5,000. One week later, John runs into an old friend. It turns out that this friend previously owned John's recently purchased car and drove it not 5,000 but 15,000 miles. Had John known this he never would have bought the car. John is the victim of the tort of misrepresentation.

There are two types of misrepresentation: deceit and

negligent misrepresentation. Simply stated, *deceit*, or fraudulent misrepresentation, is a false statement of an important
and existing fact. The actor must know that his statement is
false. He must make the statement to induce the victim to
rely on its truthfulness. The victim must suffer injury because he reasonably relied on the statement's truthfulness.
Negligent misrepresentation, on the other hand, is the making of a false statement which the speaker does not know or
even believe to be untrue, but which is made nevertheless on
the basis of no reasonable grounds.

The false statement may be oral, written, or by conduct.
A seller may explicitly tell the buyer of certain goods that he
owns them. By accepting money deposited with it, a bank
represents that it is solvent. Both the seller's words and the
bank's conduct assert statements which if not true are misrepresentations.

So-called half-truths are also misrepresentations. We are
all familiar with statements, especially in the business world,
that are true as far as they go but do not tell the whole story.
A seller who tells the buyer of a hotel the hotel's yearly income but deliberately does not disclose that a recent police
raid has severely reduced profits is liable for deceit.

Words or conduct may affirmatively conceal the truth.
This is the classic "cover-up." When a seller of a house covers
defects with plaster and paint, he has made a false statement.
Likewise, an employer has made a false statement when he
omits part of his employee's contract while reading it to the
employee. Any statement that prevents ascertaining the
truth is also a false statement.

For many years there was no duty upon a person to
disclose facts that might influence the other party to a transaction to otherwise reject it. Deceit did not cover those who
did not volunteer information. Ideas such as "buyer beware"
ruled harmfully supreme. For example, many times a house
seller could legally consummate a deal with a buyer while
knowing full well and not disclosing that the house was in-

fested with termites. In these situations, the buyer formerly was stuck.

Different states have created exceptions that have softened this harsh rule. Some states compel disclosure when there is a confidential or trust relationship between the actor and victim. Old friends, a lawyer and client, and a doctor and patient exemplify this type of relationship. In some states the actor must disclose major defects in the object of the transaction if it would not be discovered after an ordinary inspection.

Other states follow the "special information" exception, which has gone far to eviscerate the general rule. Under this exception the actor has a duty to disclose when he possesses special knowledge that the victim cannot obtain. The actor knows that without this knowledge the victim cannot possibly make an intelligent decision. The seller now, for example, must disclose that a house for sale is infested with termites.

The false statements communicated to the victim or information withheld from him must be important. The falsehood must be so significant that the victim probably would not have gone through with the transaction had he known the true facts.

The actor also must make the false statement intending to deceive the victim. He must either know the statement is false or make the statement in reckless disregard of the truth. The latter requirement means that when the actor communicates to the victim a false statement whose truth or falsehood the actor could ascertain, he has the actual intent to deceive. This imposes a duty on the actor to make a reasonable investigation to determine whether his statement is true or false.

The victim on his part must show that he justifiably relied on the truth of the actor's false statement. This means that the actor's misrepresentation was the main cause inducing the victim's course of action. It need not, however, be the only cause.

The victim's reliance on the misrepresentation cannot be foolhardy or ludicrous. If a person with ordinary intelligence, experience, and education would not be deceived, then the victim will not be compensated for injuries he sustained. One who buys the Empire State Building for a thousand dollars from someone claiming ownership is not reasonable. However, if the actor knows of a particular flaw in the victim, such as gullibility, ignorance, or illiteracy, he will not be permitted to take advantage of it. One who "sells" the Empire State Building to an imbecile is not allowed to retain his ill-gotten gain.

The false statement must pertain to a fact. Opinions communicated by the actor may not be the subject of a misrepresentation suit. The reason for this is that an opinion expresses only one point of view, which may be completely wrong. The question then arises, what is an opinion?

Opinion

Exaggerated sales talk is mere *opinion*. When salesmen bombard a customer with adjectives describing their products such as "the best," "good," or "pride of our line," the customer should be on guard. It is unreasonable to believe that a man whose livelihood depends on the number of vegetable slicers he sells offers anything more than his opinion when he puffily describes the product as "the greatest."

Communications of value are also opinions. Property is worth different amounts to different people. However, an expert's opinion on which the victim has relied is more than ordinary opinion. An expert coin collector's or dealer's appraisal of a coin's value in effect is a statement of fact.

False statements regarding the actor's intentions may in some states be sufficient for deceit. Here, the fact exists that the actor intends to do something. When someone buys goods on credit without the slightest intention of paying for them, he has committed deceit.

DEFAMATION

Defamation is a tort against a victim's reputation. It requires a false statement communicated to someone other than the victim. The statement must present the victim in a way that disgraces him in the eyes of a substantial portion of his community peers.

The statements may be by words, photographs, caricatures, drawings, signs, advertisements, or other methods. Oral defamatory statements are termed *slander*. Written statements are termed *libel*.

Anyone alive may be defamed; the dead cannot be defamed. Corporations have no personal reputation, but as their business success depends in large part on their reputation for such characteristics as honesty, efficiency, and credit, statements impugning these attributes may be defamatory.

Generally, there is no defamation if the statement refers to a large group. The remark "all doctors are quacks," even if made to a doctor, is not sufficiently particular to any one doctor to be defamation. The statement "all doctors working in the city of Lynn at 110 Main Street are quacks" probably is defamatory because the group referred to is small and definite. A doctor working at this address can show that the statement applied personally to him.

Among those who can be held liable for defamation are: the original speaker or writer of the defamation; a publisher of books, magazines, or records containing defamation; and one who repeats a defamatory statement he has heard or read. A newsstand operator or bookseller is not liable for defamation contained in materials he distributes unless he knew or had reason to know of the defamation.

The defamatory statement must be conveyed to someone other than the person defamed. The third person may be anyone, as long as he understands the defamatory nature of the statement. One who repeats defamation, regardless of what disclaimers he makes, is liable for his statement. In most states, all copies of the same printed material are treated as one communication. A person defamed in a book whose circulation numbers 50,000 can bring only one lawsuit and not 50,000.

A substantial portion of the victim's community must believe the statement that disgraced the victim. This portion need not be purely mathematical. Defamation does not depend on what percentage of a community believes the statement. Rather, it depends on the nature and quality of the community. The community may be composed of a small but well-respected membership.

We have said that slander is defamation communicated orally. For a victim to recover compensation for the injury to his reputation he must prove special monetary injury. That is, he must show that as a result of the defamation, he has somehow lost revenue.

Certain exceptions permit a victim to recover without proving a money loss. There is no need to show a money loss when the slander accuses the victim of (1) a crime of immorality, such as sodomy; (2) carrying disease, such as gonorrhea; or (3) something that will injure his business, trade, profession, or office, such as calling a surgeon a butcher.

Some slanderous communications are obviously harmful to the victim. They are susceptible to only one interpretation, which is defamatory. There are other statements which, if communicated without someone knowing more, are not slanderous. In this situation, the victim must show outside facts that show why the statement is defamatory. He must also show that the statement applied to him.

As we have mentioned, libel is written slander. To recover compensation, loss of money does not have to be proven.

Just as certain defenses of privilege exonerated actors who committed intentional torts, so too defenses of privilege may exonerate an actor who commits defamation. There are two types of privileges, absolute and qualified. Absolute privileges totally avoid an actor's liability. They are limited to statements made on the legislative floor by legislators and in court by judges, parties, witnesses, and attorneys when the statements pertain to the lawsuit. True statements also avoid all liability.

Qualified privileges are those that may be asserted by an actor who communicates the defamation without the intent to be malicious. In some states, a person may defame another as a means of self-defense to protect his reputation. In other states, he may defame to recover stolen property.

A qualified privilege exists for one to defame another to protect a group of which he is a member. A citizen who mistakenly informs police that a specific person committed a crime is not liable for defamation if he made the statement without the intent to defame. The statement must be made only to those who have a right to hear it, such as to policemen. If the actor broadcasts the statements to those who have no business to hear it, such as bystanders, malice may be implied, and he may be liable.

Anyone may say anything about the way a public officer conducts his office unless the statement is made with knowledge that it is false or in reckless disregard of whether it is true or not.

NUISANCE

Every person with an interest in land may exercise exclusive control over his land. This control must, however, be reasonable. The use of the land must not constitute a *nuisance*, causing any unnecessary annoyance or damage to his neighbors. One's use of land may not be illegal or unwarranted, nor may it produce significant discomfort, hurt, or inconvenience.

Location of the Nuisance

The location of a nuisance is often a crucial factor. A factory emitting large quantities of black smoke and soot causing laundry discoloration and air pollution will not be a nuisance if located in many of the industrial areas of Pittsburgh, Pennsylvania. Pittsburgh is an urban area producing steel. Its citizens may not like living in an uncomfortable environment, but social utility demands that the steel mills remain open. To close down the mills deprives thousands of people of jobs and payrolls; the tax base decreases, as does the purchase of supplies. The disparity in economic consequences is huge. Pittsburgh could not survive without the steel industry. Ultimately, a court would have to decide whether the benefits of removing steel mills outweigh its detriments.

On the other hand, if the smoke- and soot-emitting factory were located in Yellowstone National Park, it undoubtedly would be a nuisance. The park is used for the specific purpose of affording nature lovers the chance to see a preindustrialized environment. Any enterprise interfering with an individual's enjoyment of nature in this situation would be stopped. There can be only one location for Yellowstone Park, while there are many possible locations for a factory. It is not reasonable for a factory to destroy this naturalist preserve.

The Nature of the Nuisance Injury

Generally, the injury inflicted by the nuisance must be tangible, irreparable, recurring often, and incapable of monetary evaluation. The victim must be harmed in fact, not in mere conjecture. Special sensitivities of the victim are irrelevant. When a church bell is constantly rung near the home of a highly nervous individual, there is no nuisance. Ringing a church bell is a reasonable activity.

The Cost of Ameliorating or Eliminating the Nuisance. The cost of ameliorating or eliminating the nuisance ought to be commensurate with the harm it causes. If the cost of eliminating the discharge of factory waste that injures fish is monetarily astronomical (and would put the owners out of business) compared to the number of fish harmed, then the factory might be permitted to continue operation. A court would balance the interests in maintaining the factory with those of protecting fish. A five-million-dollar factory probably will not be closed down because some fish are harmed. At bottom, a judgment must be made as to what is more important: a factory or sea life.

Curing the Nuisance

A court will usually give the person creating the nuisance an opportunity to reduce its effects on the victim to a tolerable level. This factor must be considered with the previous one just discussed, because frequently much money must be used for technical research or equipment that will abate the nuisance. Certain nuisances cannot be abated by any equipment, and research into abating the problem is not helpful. A good-faith effort to improve conditions by the creator of the nuisance, even if it is futile, may work in his favor.

From what we have just discussed, it should be clear that no one factor will determine whether an interference with enjoyment of land is a nuisance. Often the listed factors conflict with one another. In that case, a court will balance the overall harm to the nuisance-maker in forcing him to stop the nuisance with the benefit to the victim when the nuisance ends.

It is irrelevant that the victim came to the nuisance. If, in a twenty-year period, a community of 30,000 people grew up around a factory whose pollution is severe, a judge will not take into consideration the fact that the factory existed before people arrived in determining whether the factory is a nuisance. Should he find that it is a nuisance, he may force the residents to bear the cost of the factory's relocation if they want it shut down.

We have stated that the injury sustained by the victim must be incapable of monetary evaluation. When a neighbor's howling dogs prevent a homeowner from sleeping at night, the homeowner generally does not want money for his trouble; he wants a good night's rest. Should he go to court seeking monetary compensation, the court is forced to make a virtually impossible evaluation of how much money a good night's rest is worth. Money is not too helpful because the homeowner really wants his neighbor to silence the dogs. He wants the judge to tell his neighbor to keep the dogs quiet or spend some time in jail until he does. This type of help from the court is termed *injunctive relief*.

An *injunction* is a direction from a court to a person ordering him to do or not to do something. It is used when money compensation will not help the victim. When a factory is judged to be a nuisance because of smoke, dirt, and dust emissions, its neighbors do not primarily want money (although they may want money to pay for medical expenses incurred because of the pollution); they want the factory to stop polluting. An injunction will fulfill their desire. Generally, injunctions are the main relief granted to victims of nuisance.

INTERFERENCE WITH CONTRACTUAL RELATIONS

One may not interfere with a contract between parties unless he is privileged to do so. The contract must be in existence at the time of the interference. It must not be illegal.

The manner of interference may be by causing one party to the contract to breach. A theater owner who induces a star opera singer under contract to his competitor to breach the contract has committed the tort. Interference may be by causing one party's performance of his part of the contract to increase in cost or to become more burdensome. Deliberately damaging a television set that the victim is under contract to repair makes the actor liable.

One is privileged to interfere with a contractual relation if he can show justification for the interference. Interference motivated by malice generally is not justified. The actor will be justified in his interference if he can show that he acted to further a proper purpose. A high school principal may cause a teacher to be fired by showing the teacher to be engaged in illegal conduct.

An actor may interfere to protect his existing economic interest. For example, a store owner may prevent the previous owner of the store from working for a competitor across the street if the contract of sale states that the previous owner would not compete with the new owner. In every case the interference itself may not be tortious. One who is justified to interfere may not do so by committing false imprisonment or battery.

LIABILITY FOR TORTS

Parental Liability for Child's Tort

Parents may be liable for their children's torts only because of either the parents' negligence or their failure to properly exercise their power of control over the children. Parents may be negligent in permitting their children to play with or otherwise use dangerous articles that injure others. Parents may likewise be negligent by not confiscating dangerous articles that their children have shown a history of misusing, such as matches or a car or a toy gun. In all these instances, the parents are liable along with the children.

Parents have a special power of control over their children. This control must be exercised to prevent injury to others. To be liable, the parent must have notice of the harmful conduct the child has a tendency to commit and an opportunity to prevent the conduct.

In most instances, however, parents are not liable for the torts of their children. When Johnnie gets into a fight after school, his parents are not going to be held liable for injuries the other child suffered in the fight. Only when Johnnie used the knife his parents gave him for Christmas would the parents be potentially liable.

Statute of Limitations

Statutes of Limitations are time limits within which a victim of an injury must sue for damages. Generally, a victim has two or three years from the time he discovers the injury to sue. However, this period has been greatly varied by statute.

Immunities

Certain persons or entities, because of their relation to society in general or the victim in particular, are immune from tort liability.

The ancient idea of sovereign immunity, which originated with the concept that you could not sue the king, for a long time prevented tort suits against the United States government or its employees acting on behalf of the government. However, the United States has waived this right of sovereign immunity and may now be sued for negligent torts committed by its employees while acting within the scope of their employment. On the other hand, the Federal Government is not liable for intentional torts caused by employees. Many suits against the United States are controlled by statutes, and a lawyer should be consulted to determine if a suit will be proper.

The Eleventh Amendment to the United States Constitution prohibits citizens from suing any of the fifty states. However, this immunity has been waived in varying degrees by all states.

Charities are totally immune from tort liability only in a very few states. Some states deny immunity to charities but, by statute, limit the amount a victim can receive as compensation. No fewer than thirty-one states have abolished charitable immunity completely. Clearly, the trend of the law is moving toward abolition or extreme limitation of most forms of governmental and charitable immunities.

Since everyone may be subject to a tortious lawsuit, it is incumbent upon each person to understand his rights and responsibilities within a civil society both to protect himself against a suit and to be accurately aware of his rights and powers as a citizen.

7

Your Consumer Rights

What is a "consumer"? Most usually, the word "consumer" is used to describe someone like you or me, who purchases goods for primarily personal, family, or household purposes. Although corporations, merchants, businesses, wholesalers, and the like are purchasers of goods, the word "consumer" applies only to the "little guy" who buys goods for use in his or her home. The word also can apply to purchasers of services—as in hiring a repairperson to fix your TV—and to renters of apartments, housing, and even space for mobile homes. As you can see, the definition of consumer is not rigid, but can be used to describe a great variety of commercial transactions.

The nineteenth century in this country saw the shaping of the philosophy of *caveat emptor*, "let the buyer beware." Under this individualistic, pro-seller maxim, courts offered little help to the victims of inequitable sales transactions, except in the case of outright fraud. Buyers were presumed to be on their guard whenever they entered into contracts to buy any kind of product or service.

By the end of the first half of the twentieth century, however, with the incredible rise in the consumption of consumer goods in this country—and the attendant rise in consumer *problems*—courts were struggling to limit the harsh effect of the doctrine of *caveat emptor*. Consumers came to be viewed as all-too-frequent victims of overreaching merchants and remote, impersonal corporate sellers.

But the case-by-case response of the courts to consumer problems soon proved to be of limited help to the growing number of American consumers. Our vast marketplace was changing in leaps and bounds, and the courts were not keeping in step. Thus, by the early part of this century it became obvious that the only appropriate solution to these problems would be government regulation—by federal and state statutes and local ordinances and through the creation of special federal, state, and municipal agencies. This public regulation of private commercial transactions has been the watchtower of consumer protection in this country in recent times. Most states have established consumer protection bureaus within either the attorney general's or the governor's offices, and several states have instituted independent departments of consumer affairs. Moreover, today nearly forty federal agencies play some part in consumer protection.

Most states have enacted broadly defined consumer protection laws, which outlaw "unfair or deceptive trade practices." These illegal-seller practices may take the form either of deceptive practices that tend to mislead consumers or of outright deceitful and fraudulent practices in which the seller knowingly and intentionally engages. Let us take a look at the most common consumer grievances concerning seller practices and then see what remedies (means employed to enforce a right or to redress a violation of that right) are available to consumers generally.

VOID OR VOIDABLE CONSUMER CONTRACTS

A contract for the sale of goods worth more than $500 must be in writing. But whether or not a formal sales contract is drawn up, you should know that if either the merchant or private individual seller engages in certain conduct before the deal is made, then the agreement is "tainted" or "voidable," that is, you have the option of getting out of the deal if you wish. When a seller knowingly makes a fraudulent misrepresentation about an important aspect of the product—for example, a dishwasher that the salesperson knows to be fifteen years old is misrepresented as five years old—that is sufficient grounds to void (invalidate) the sales agreement. But bear in mind that mere "puffing" or "sales talk," such as "This model is selling like hotcakes," does not constitute fraudulent misrepresentation.

Under most consumer protection laws, a consumer also can get out of a sales agreement where it can be shown that the seller was guilty of an unfair or deceptive practice—for example, where a vacuum cleaner advertised for $69.69 proves to be unusable without an additional $19.99 part.

An unconscionable contract is one in which the seller, through flagrant overreaching in the bargaining process, has taken grossly unfair advantage of the consumer. An example would be a contract for the sale of a refrigerator worth $300, but for which the consumer eventually must pay $900 after all the charges and interest have been included. In all states, such a contract would be voidable on the part of the consumer.

A contract to buy consumer goods also can be set aside if the buyer was underage, mentally incompetent, or intoxicated when he or she entered into the agreement. You will remember that these exceptions actually apply to all contracts. Thus, if the merchant is not registered to do business in the state, or if the contract otherwise violates specific local statutes covering sales transactions, the agreement is rendered a nullity. And if a mutual mistake occurred—suppose that both you and the seller mistook a 1963 VW for a 1964 model—then neither of you is bound by the contract. (See chapter on contracts.)

Consumer Remedies

When you attempt to void (invalidate) a consumer contract, you are trying to get out of the deal and pay no money at all, collect damages (money compensation for your loss because of the unlawful act of another) from the merchant, or both. Your first step should be a strongly worded letter to the seller, explaining in detail what trouble you have experienced and asking him or her to rectify the problem. Send the letter by certified mail, return receipt requested, and keep a carbon copy for your records. If the response you get is unsatisfactory, you should ask your local Better Business Bureau or consumer agency (if there is one) to intercede for you. If all this fails, you will have to hire a lawyer to sue in court for the disaffirmance of the contract and possibly for damages.

If your complaint is that the seller misrepresented some important piece of information or engaged in a deceptive practice, you must consult with an attorney, a legal services organization, or a consumer agency to determine: first, if your state has a formal set of consumer protection laws; and, second, if you have sufficient grounds to bring a consumer fraud action (lawsuit) against the seller.

If you believe you were taken advantage of under an unconscionable contract, you must sue to obtain a court judgment releasing you from the agreement. A widespread and particularly outrageous seller practice may warrant a class action brought by a group of aggrieved consumers; you also may petition the attorney general of your state to take action on behalf of this group. (Revocation of state licensing is a powerful regulatory mechanism.)

AUTOMOBILES

The most common consumer gripe anywhere is the "lemon"—that new or used car that turns out to be more of an aggravation than a convenience. The automobile may be one of the most important and expensive purchases a person ever makes, but it is a transaction fraught with potential costly and time-consuming problems.

That brand-new car you bought from your local new car dealer last week already may be back in the dealer's garage because of one or more defective parts or because some feature on the car was missing or failed to conform to your expectations. That used car you just purchased may have failed to make it through the first week, or you may have discovered that the previous owner failed to disclose some essential information about the car—for example, the fact that the odometer had been turned back or that the car originally had been used as a police car, taxi, or rental car. All these seller practices and others may be illegal under the consumer protection laws of your state.

You probably financed the purchase of your car through the car dealership directly, through a finance company formed by the car's manufacturer (for example, GMAC, Chrysler Credit), or through a loan from a bank or small loan company. Under the terms of the finance or credit agreement you signed, the creditor (lender) takes a security interest in your car and the right to repossess it if you (debtor) default on the payments. In return, the creditor loans you capital for the purchase price of the automobile, allowing you to pay for it on time. In regard to this finance agreement, you should ask yourself the following questions:

Was I given the opportunity to read the entire contract—even the "small print"—before I signed it?

Were all parts of the contract printed in "readable" type?

Were the creditor's right of repossession and my payment obligations understandable?

Were any oral representations made to me by the creditor incorporated into the written agreement?

If you answer "No" to any of these questions, the circumstances surrounding this credit transaction arguably were suspect.

Automobile Consumer Remedies

The best protection against a defective car is prevention. Always have a mechanic check the vehicle over before you buy it. However, even the most thorough inspection may fail to uncover a hidden defect. You should notify the seller in writing immediately of all defects and keep copies of your letters.

All automobile manufacturers issue a written warranty, which is a written promise that the character and quality of the product are as the manufacturer represents them to be. This warranty guarantees that, within a specified number of miles or period of months, the manufacturer and, if so specified, its registered dealers will replace or repair defective parts at no cost, as long as the defect was not the fault of the consumer. Some dealers may be reluctant to honor warranties because they may receive only partial reimbursement from the manufacturer, but a failure to honor a warranty could constitute an unfair or deceptive trade practice under the consumer protection laws in your state.

The sale of any consumer good, including automobiles, carries with it implied warranties. Implied warranties are not written but are inherent in the transaction. The two most widely used implied warranties are the warranty of merchantability (salability and fitness for the market—for example, a toaster that doesn't "pop" would be unmerchantable) and fitness for a particular purpose (a pair of shoes that the seller knows will be used for mountain climbing must be fit for that purpose). Most automobile warranties contain "disclaimers" (denials, disavowals) of these implied warranties and any other express warranties. But you should know that, under both the Uniform Commercial Code, which has been adopted fairly uniformly in all states but Louisiana, and the Consumer Product Warranty Act, a federal statute enacted in 1975, any disclaimer of implied warranties must be conscionable (just) and must be written in simple, easily understandable, and conspicuous language. If your automobile warranty does not conform to these standards, you may be able to sue the manufacturer for breach of warranty and recover money damages.

If you purchased a "lemon" through a three-party credit system—(you bought the car from the seller, but you end up making payments on it to a finance company or a bank affiliated with the seller)—you may have little recourse under traditional commercial law, unless the consumer protection laws in your state specifically protect you in this area. You cannot simply refuse to make payments to the creditor. However, you at least should contact both the seller and the creditor (in writing and by certified mail, return receipt requested) and allow the seller sufficient time to correct the defect. You may choose to defend yourself in court if sued by the bank or finance company, or you may want to institute your own lawsuit against the seller and the creditor in small claims court, if your town, city, or county has one. In any event, consult with a lawyer or legal services worker as to your rights.

In any case, you must allow the dealer a reasonable amount of time to repair the defects. All new cars have imperfections, and it is only fair that the seller be allowed a reasonable number of opportunities to remedy those defects before any legal action against him can be taken.

HOUSEHOLD GOODS

As a prudent consumer, you should be aware of the many potential problems you face in purchasing an item for your own personal or household use. You always should make sure that the price you are paying for merchandise is the *agreed* price, that is, the price that the buyer and seller said when they made the deal, or the price that was given on the sales slip or receipt or in advertisements, catalogues, or tags. Moreover, this agreed price should not be inflated with any "extras" that were not made clear to you. Finally, the price you pay should not be unconscionable, that is, one that outrageously exceeds the actual value of the goods.

The goods that are delivered to your door should be as merchantable as when you paid for them in the store. If you agreed with the seller as to an exact date of delivery, the seller is bound by that agreement; and you need not tolerate late delivery. A nondelivered oven, for example, may mean days or even weeks of having to eat in restaurants. Even if you made no such agreement, the seller is obligated to deliver the goods within a reasonable time, which usually means within four weeks. In addition, you don't have to accept delivery of broken or substituted merchandise; without an agreement between the two of you to the contrary, the seller is responsible for such improper delivery.

General Consumer Remedies

If you contract to buy a good that later proves to be defective, damaged, or otherwise unacceptable, a variety of remedies are available to you under the law. If the seller fails to deliver the merchandise, or if it arrives broken, substituted, or late, you have a cause of action against the seller for breach of contract, for which you are entitled to damages to cover your loss because of the breach. Suppose, however, that the subject of the transaction is something unique, like a valuable painting. In such a case, you would be entitled to sue for specific performance, that is, the seller would be compelled to go through with the sale according to the precise terms agreed upon. Still another option available to you upon receipt of unacceptable goods or upon the seller's failure to deliver would be "covering," by buying substitute goods and suing the seller for the difference in price between the substitute goods and the contracted goods. However, the seller may have the right to "cure" the defects of any nonconforming goods within a reasonable time (which cannot be later than the agreed date for delivery, if there is one).

All the above remedies require legal assistance in their implementation. If the seller breaches either the implied warranty of merchantability or the implied warranty of fitness for a particular purpose, however, two "self-help" remedies are open to you. Under the Uniform Commercial Code, you have the right to inspect all goods before accepting them; and you may reject the defective goods in whole or in part, as long as you notify the seller at the time of delivery or within a reasonable time thereafter. If you discover that the nonconformity of the goods substantially impairs their value to you, you may notify the seller within a reasonable time after your discovery that you are revoking your acceptance; then you may get your money back by returning the goods, or else sue for damages.

Under the Fair Packaging and Labeling Act, a federal law enacted in 1966, the net contents of a package of food must be printed in a specified spot on the package. Several states have gone even further in packaging regulation by adopting *unit pricing*, pricing a food product by units of weight. Moreover, the United States Food and Drug Administration has established standards for the labeling of all drug and food products. As for clothing, it is the law that a label telling you what the product is made of must be attached to all wool, fur, and textile products; and care labels that contain laundering or drycleaning directions must appear on all garments. Contact the Washington, D.C., or regional offices of the Food and Drug Administration or the Federal Trade Commission for further appropriate information.

You should be particularly watchful of unsafe products, especially children's toys, that might explode, shatter, or otherwise cause you serious injury. The federal government has enacted various pieces of product safety legislation—the Consumer Product Safety Act, the Federal Hazardous Substances Act, the Flammable Fabrics Act, and the Refrigerator Safety Act—and has established an agency, the Consumer Product Safety Commission, to enforce these laws. If you have been seriously injured by a hazardous product, you should hire an attorney and sue the manufacturer for damages; if not, you may use one of the self-help remedies described above, return the product, and get your money back from the seller. In addition, you should try to protect other consumers by informing the Consumer Product Safety Commission in Washington, D.C. of the existence of any dangerous products.

Finally, as discussed in the section on automobiles, the 1975 Consumer Product Warranty Act affords you some protection when purchasing a household product accompanied by a warranty (for example, a washing machine). Any warranty or disclaimer thereof must be written in simple, conspicuous language and must not contain any tricky promises or guarantees. It is important that you read a warranty or disclaimer of warranty in advance and consult a knowledgeable person if you have any questions.

ADVERTISING AND PROMOTION

Merchants employ a variety of techniques to lure consumers into their stores. Most are legitimate, but some are against the law. Advertisements that merchants know to be untrue and fraudulent are undoubtedly illegal, but many unfair or deceptive promotional and advertising practices are of a much subtler nature. The "bait and switch" technique, for instance, involves an advertisement—"a complete dinette set for only $89.00," say, that is designed as tempting bait to entice a customer into the store. A salesperson then attempts to persuade the customer to buy a more expensive item. A customer who asks to see the advertised product, will be met with a variety of excuses, such as the unavailability of the product or its poor condition. The "bait and switch" is often associated with disreputable bulk-freezer-meat operators. In any event, it is an illegal practice in most states and is actionable by the relevant consumer agency in your state.

Another illegal advertising or promotional practice is false or deceptive pricing. Consumer protection laws outlaw the advertising of a selling price in comparison with another price such as "Regularly sold at $79.99, for a limited time only, $29.99," when such a comparison is untrue. If a selling price is misrepresented as the general retail price or if the manufacturer's list price is stated as wholesale or as a special introductory offer, when in fact it is not, this constitutes an unfair or deceptive trade practice.

There are a variety of other sales "pitches" of which the wise consumer should be wary. For instance, receiving unordered merchandise in the mail is a well-known seller "come-on." In addition, customers may be enticed to shop at a particular store through the promise of "easy" credit, when, in fact, the terms of the credit arrangement prove to be not easy at all but quite harsh.

Another fraudulent "come-on" is telling a person that he or she has won a contest when other conditions, such as the purchase of additional goods, must be met before the consumer receives the prize.

Similarly, offers of free merchandise that are not free or have "strings" attached is an illegal seller practice. For instance, "going-out-of-business" sales where the merchant has no intention of going out of business are prohibited. Similarly, false deceptive endorsements and claims of affiliation (for example, a false claim that a product bears the Good Housekeeping Limited Warranty seal, or an untrue claim that "We're a nonprofit organization") are illegal seller practices. The elderly are especially vulnerable to advertisers' false health and extra income claims; all too often older people are enticed to buy, for example, "cure-all" medicines for arthritis and rheumatism or invest in "fast-buck" vending machine operations.

Finally, you as a consumer should be on your guard if confronted with door-to-door, referral, or pyramid sales schemes. A consumer generally will have no recourse against a door-to-door salesperson of aluminum siding or chinchillas who proves to be a "fly-by-night"; so you should check that such a salesperson is affiliated with a well-known, reputable company.

In a referral sales scheme, a salesperson will tell you, for example, that if four of your friends agree to buy the same product, you will receive that product free; but he or she may neglect to tell you that you will have to pay the full price if only three of your friends buy it. Promoted by "multilevel distribution companies" usually associated with cosmetics and motivation courses, pyramid sales schemes offer consumers the right to sell a particular product and the right to sell that right to sell the product. The trouble is that as more people become involved in the scheme, it becomes more difficult to sell the product, and the participants are often stuck with large quantities of unwanted merchandise that they were induced to buy as "stock."

Consumer Remedies

Section 5 of the 1971 Federal Trade Commission Act and most state consumer protection laws broadly define what constitutes an "unfair or deceptive trade practice." If you feel that you've been the victim of an artful con, you should contact the nearest consumer agency to determine if you have a good case for rescinding (setting aside) the sales contract. More and more courts are applying the doctrine of strict liability in cases of knowing and intentional misrepresentation. Liability is imposed on the defendant without fault and without defenses to save him. If you've been the victim of a widespread, repeated practice, you may, as previously suggested, wish to join other identifiable consumers in a consumer class action to redress individually small but virtually identical damages claims.

Under a Federal Trade Commission rule concerning door-to-door consumer credit transactions, a door-to-door salesperson must provide you with a readable copy of the contract (in your native tongue) and a "Notice of Cancellation" form. You then have a three-day "cooling off" period in which to think the deal over and cancel the transaction without any obligation to you. Sometimes known as a "Buyer's Remorse Law," this FTC rule gives you the unilateral right to rescind the credit sales contract if these standards are not met and you do not receive the cancellation form.

SERVICES

The consumer protection laws in most states cover personal services along with tangible goods. The term *services* can range in meaning from home repairs and improvements—the TV repairperson, the plumber, and the painter, for example—to professional services—the lawyer, the doctor, and the funeral director—to employment agencies and vocational and training schools.

Most consumer complaints in this area concern shoddy or dishonest repair work. To avoid the many problems wrought by unprofessional or even unscrupulous repairpeople, you should recognize the danger signs of unfair or deceptive repair work. A repairperson who refuses to give you an estimate at your request is acting unfairly and perhaps even illegally, depending on the law in your state. The bill the repairperson eventually renders you should be itemized and clearly understandable, with no overcharges, undisclosed service charges, or charges for unnecessary or unauthorized repairs.

Professionals may be the source of many consumer complaints, but often people are too trusting of or too intimidated by professionals to air their dissatisfaction. Nevertheless, a prevalent grievance concerning professionals is that they overcharge for the amount of work they produce. Another less frequent but no less valid accusation against some professionals is that they are guilty of malpractice. Consumers also complain of delay on the part of their lawyers, failure to inform and explain on the part of their physicians and dentists, and prohibitive and unnecessary costs charged by their funeral directors.

Two other services that have the potential for creating many costly problems for the consumer are employment agencies and vocational and training schools. Eager, unsuspecting job-seekers who have engaged for a fee the services of employment agencies have reported that some unscrupulous agencies failed to find them a suitable job or *any* job; they have accused other agencies of discrimination and false advertising.

Like employment agencies, private vocational and training schools have been charged with engaging in unfair or deceptive advertising practices. For example, they may lead students to believe that enrollment in the school guarantees them of a high-paying job after graduation, when in fact such a promise is extremely unrealistic. Some vocational students also have complained that they were pressured into taking courses they didn't want, that they couldn't get refunds for courses they dropped, and that they were dissatisfied with the quality of the teaching.

Consumer Remedies for Services

Always attempt to negotiate a settlement of your dispute with a repairperson before taking any legal action. If your efforts prove fruitless and you believe the repairperson's conduct was unfair or deceptive, consult with a lawyer to see if you have grounds to sue for damages for violation of the state consumer protection laws.

Another effective remedy at your disposal against flagrant infractions is to file a written complaint with the particular state licensing board involved. Unfortunately, however, no state requires licensing of automobile mechanics; if a mechanic merely bungles the job and commits no deceptive or unfair act, you have no legal recourse.

In the case of professionals, a telephone call or visit probably will resolve the problem. If your complaint is malpractice, however, you should contemplate instituting a lawsuit; at the very least you should contact the state board of registration involved (for example, the state bar association or the state medical or dental society) and complain of the professional's gross misconduct.

As employment agencies and vocational and training schools also must be registered with the state, you should address any complaints about these services to their respective state licensing boards, as well as to the local Chamber of Commerce or Better Business Bureau. It is always good advice to get the facts *before* engaging either of these services. Talk to potential employers, career counselors at local or state employment agencies, and trade associations. In addition, if the consumer is a veteran or serviceman, he may want to talk with the regional Veterans Administration office.

CREDIT

Nearly every major consumer transaction into which you enter involves credit in some form or another, whether it means writing a check for a percolator, using your credit card to buy a new dress, taking out a car loan, or buying life insurance. There are basically two kinds of credit: "open-end" or "revolving" credit includes credit cards (American Express, Visa, Master Charge) and store charge accounts. "Closed-end" or "straight" credit means a bank or loan company loan for a particular good or service (probably an automobile) or an installment loan (for, say, aluminum siding), under an "installment" or "conditional" sales contract.

Probably the most common consumer complaint in the area of credit is that the creditor (lender) failed to explain the total credit costs of the transaction. Total costs are what the consumer ends up paying in interest and other charges in addition to the principal sum of the loan or balance of the account. Other consumers have accused loan companies and banks of misleading advertising, which usually promises "easy" credit that turns out to be far from easy. Furthermore, if you are a woman or a member of a minority group, you may have been discriminated against in applying for credit. If you are in default on your installment payments, you may find that your "friendly" credit company feels no compunction about sending debt collectors to knock on your door and repossess the merchandise you bought on credit. Finally, you should always be wary of mail-order insurance business. Especially, don't be fooled by veteran and Medicare policies, which are legitimately offered only by the United States Government.

Credit Consumer Remedies
Your rights and liabilities in credit sales are complicated matters. It is therefore best to seek expert legal advice before entering into any important transaction or if any action such as repossession, attachment (seizing a debtor's property to satisfy a debt), or garnishment (diversion of a portion of your weekly paycheck to the creditor) is taken against you. But you should be aware of three important federal laws that protect the individual consumer seeking credit. Under the Truth-in-Lending Law, passed by Congress in 1968, in any

consumer credit transaction under $25,000 the lender must prominently display in advertisements the finance charge and annual percentage rate (APR) and must explain to the borrower how much he or she owes and how much he or she must pay. Otherwise, the entire transaction may be voidable.

In determining what kind of credit risk you are, most creditors use computerized "files," or credit reports on you, which show, for example, how you pay your bills, if you've ever filed for bankruptcy or been sued or arrested, and so on. These reports may even contain opinions of your neighbors and friends as to your reputation or manner of living. Under the Fair Credit Reporting Act, passed by Congress in 1971 to protect consumers against the circulation of erroneous information about them in credit reports, you have the right to know what consumer reporting agency prepared the report on you that was used to deny you credit. You also are entitled to obtain a copy of this report and to correct any erroneous, obsolete, frivolous, or incomplete information.

Finally, the Equal Credit Opportunity Act prohibits creditors from discriminating on the basis of sex, marital status, race, color, religion, national origin, and age in any aspect of a credit transaction. If you are a woman, you should know that a creditor may not consider your sex, marital status, age, or child-bearing plans in evaluating your credit-worthiness. If you have a complaint under any of these three federal statutes, you may be able to sue the creditor and collect damages. Consult your state attorney general's office or the nearest Federal Trade Commission Office.

REGULATED INDUSTRIES

Consumers rely on the services of government-regulated public utilities—the water, gas, electric, and telephone companies—for many vital daily activities; yet these services have been the cause of much customer dissatisfaction. You should familiarize yourself with the methods by which the utility companies measure your consumption, and you always should check the accuracy of your bill. Other "bones" of contention with these companies have centered around the unreasonable requirement of deposits and around termination of services without notification or under disputed circumstances.

If you've ever engaged the services of a household moving company, you may have been none too pleased with the movers' packing and unpacking of your possessions, which might have resulted in the scratching of furniture or the damage to your one-of-a-kind tea service. You may not have known the extent of the moving company's liability for damage or loss of your household goods; you probably were unaware of the high risk of storing your goods in warehouses at either end of the trip.

A fertile source of consumer "rip-offs" has been chartered air travel. Unfortunately, most of the problems connected with chartered flights manifest themselves after the travelers have embarked on their trip. It is usually after the flight arrives at its destination—when the travelers are virtually stranded—that they discover that their hotel accommodations are unsatisfactory or even nonexistent or that a return flight has not been booked.

Consumer Remedies for Regulated Industries

Any complaints about public utilities should be brought up first with the individual company. Many public utility companies (and other industries, as well) sponsor consumer action panels to resolve consumer grievances. If you can't settle your dispute in this fashion, file a grievance with your local or state department of public utilities. Some state consumers' councils (such as those in Massachusetts, Rhode Island, and New Jersey) are authorized by law to represent consumer interests in all public utility department and rate-setting commission proceedings.

Interstate moving companies come under the jurisdiction of the Interstate Commerce Commission, a federal agency. Like the Federal Trade Commission, the ICC has its headquarters in Washington, D.C., and several regional offices around the country. In the case of intrastate moves, seek the aid of your state attorney general's office or department of public utilities.

If you've experienced a charter flight "rip-off," complain to the airline carrier, hotel, or other defaulting service. If you are abroad, contact the closest United States consulate or embassy. With serious and frequent consumer problems involving air carriers, contact the Office of Consumer Affairs of the Civil Aeronautics Board in Washington, D.C.; the CAB is responsible for licensing airlines that provide charter flights.

CONCLUSION

The days of *caveat emptor*—"let the buyer beware"—fortunately have faded away. American courts have come to realize that, no matter how careful you are in buying and no matter how thoroughly you inspect merchandise before accepting it, you have no way of protecting yourself against some defective goods. Nowadays the courts have equipped consumers with a panoply of means to redress the negligence and lack of due care of merchants or dealers, their employees, and even the manufacturer doing business hundreds of miles away.

Consumer protection has expanded rapidly in the last quarter-century. Consumer bureaus have sprung up in most states, and dozens of federal agencies have joined in the fight against faulty mass-production consumer goods. Unquestionably, the 1960s and 1970s have seen the increasing involvement of federal, state, and local government in consumer transactions. But remember that *you*, as an individual, often can get completely satisfactory results on your own if you take a firm stand against unfair or deceptive seller practices. Complain to the management, write strongly worded letters, return the merchandise—but never take a consumer fraud lying down. Much of the law is on *your* side now as the consumer, but the guilty party is not going to invoke these laws on your behalf. Commencing the action to stand up for your rights can only be done by you.

8

The Legal Rights Of Minorities

It is traditionally the people in control of society who determine for those with less power what their self-image will be. It has been proven in numerous studies that children who are persistently told that they are bright attain a higher level of achievement than children who are told nothing at all. The principle behind this result consistently determines what the rights of each and every minority will be at any given point in time.

THE INTENTIONAL PERPETUATION OF INEQUALITY

Among many black families victimized by centuries of the "white is right" psychosis, children with lighter skin pigmentation until recently had been presumed to be the brightest and were raised on that presumption. Given encouragement, books, praise, and a belief that what was expected of them could potentially be realized, lighter-skinned children more often did achieve more than darker children who were offered less hope and less belief in a positive self-image.

With this demonstrable success, the senseless myth could be perpetuated with justification and reality; and attempts to show why it happens and how it could be changed to give everyone an equal chance at success fell on ears that were deaf, unwilling, or unable to understand the root causes of inequality.

It is likewise true that more women are physically and mentally handicapped than men in many areas of their lives, not because they were born less capable, but because from birth girls have been told repeatedly that a woman cannot do this or that, a woman's place is at home, and that females should not be aggressive. Strength is not "feminine" in a world where men are the gender designated for leadership, for achievement, for dominance.

Accordingly, the twentieth-century Western woman's self-perception as powerless but meant-to-be-pretty has been reinforced by those with power, the men in society they have been conditioned to serve. Males wrote the books on psychology that condemned women who deviated; they dictated the financial dependence of women, and they ruled the sexual roost. It has been successful for most of the West's modern history because the cycle was never broken, and the oppressed thought of herself as the oppressor had defined her. By design, she knew no better, even going to the point of echoing the condemnations of those who tried to show her lack of freedom.

Those same psychologists have, in our modern culture, told people who participated in physical love with the same sex that they were sick, deviant, and unworthy of any legal protection. As human beings, they have been arrested, put away for years, fired from their jobs, and displaced from their homes simply because of the way they participated in the very private act of sex. As with darker-skinned children and women, it did not matter what a person could do or in fact had achieved who was sexually attracted to the same sex, irrespective of the stability, reliability, or vocational capabilities of that person.

Because they are different from what continues to be erroneously perceived as the majority, people with same-sex attractions were and are mocked and singled out for persecution. As it is very difficult to spot most people on the basis of what they do in their bedrooms, persecution was reserved for that minority within a minority which was most visible to the alleged majority.

The treatment of same-sex partners who had been told since their age of awareness that they were not whole people, that they were "sissies" if born a man and "butch" if born a woman, inevitably has resulted in some people becoming living manifestations of the images in which they were perceived. Out of either a need to identify or a defensiveness against ostracism, some men became limp-wristed, meek, bitchy, and lisping of speech; and some women became aggressive, physically imposing, and even ferocious.

These types were only a small segment within a much larger but invisible minority, and their existence was due to the majority powers determining that minority's image of itself. Conforming to negative stereotyping, this visible segment of the significant minority of the population has been meted out the irrational abuse always reserved for those in a society with the least ability to retaliate. Through discrimination in every conceivable facet of life, these people have been rendered typically powerless, more so even than the American black, and their self-image has fallen into line accordingly.

As for the alleged majority, it turns against these and other minorities from a defensiveness of its own. A recent

government study concluded that the overwhelming majority of American homes were not operating within the struc-
ture of a working father and a mother-housewife taking care
of their children at home. Most individual citizens of this
nation thus have had to stuff down secret fears that they
were abnormal, as they watched fictitious models played by
Robert Young, Jane Wyatt, and Ozzie and Harriet Nelson.

Most people were not about to concede that they were
not in the American mainstream, as happy as Ozzie, as secure
as David and Ricky. Rather than free themselves from this
guilt, they collectively aligned themselves with what they perceived and was perceived for them as the good majority and
continue today to unwittingly aid and abet the powered in
manipulating their own lives and ambitions.

And so if "Father Knows Best" and Ozzie Nelson have
"that kind" of home and family, *that* is the mold to which the
middle-class American feels he must conform. He may not
be comfortable as a married man or a business man or a
parent, but he will try, because he does not know that Ozzie
Nelson and Robert Young are acting and are sponsored by
industries whose profits depend upon increased con-
sumerism that is based upon a deception about the actual
condition of things.

Even if he grasps that he doesn't fit into this alleged
majority mold, he is unaware that, by not fitting, he is actually *in* the majority and that what he incorrectly sees as the
majority is largely a myth, even according to our government. He acts on an image that tells him that if he follows
certain paths he can achieve a degree of upward mobility that
will bring him at least nearer the realization of the delusion
of a better life.

He spends his productive years conforming to that
myth, instead of being allowed to adjust comfortably to who
he actually is; and in the process he tries to put some distance
between himself and those others in society he thinks are a
minority and therefore less worthy of approval. Progress,

like all movement, is relative only to the positions by and from which we measure.

LACK OF UPWARD MOBILITY

These positions in society, or *sociological stratifications*, have their foundations built upon the sands of each person's ability to move upwards. It is perceived on a subconscious level that the more distance one can put between oneself and others the more progress one will make. Of course, this logic is fallacious, because when people do not feel they can move upward in a society and are trapped on a low level of stratification, they have no vested stake in the maintenance of order in that society.

Minority races also form a contrast against which the majority measures its fictitious worth. Much as one would not know that an ocean wave were high without smaller waves with which to contrast it, whites (or unisexuals or men) could not see themselves as superior unless there were lower groups. Keeping minorities down serves this purpose, and it is in the self-interest of the majority to retain this status through intentional oppression.

The results of maintaining nonmobile classes are omnipresent today. Having little chance of achieving what they have seen on television every night and being told they are "dumb niggers," "faggots," "helpless broads," and "thuggy kids," minorities have conformed to that image. It is much the way that the child who is told he is bright conforms in a positive sense to that preconception, thereby making it a valid conclusion. With no impetus or hope to move upwards, they have turned to crime, drugs, welfare, and aggression. Even those suburbanites who perceive themselves as able to progress are making no progress at all, because keeping down some people is keeping down everyone; and crime, drugs, welfare, and aggression are ruining the quality of life for us all. Afraid to move out of their homes at night, white Americans refuse to give out the candles they possess and opt for a nonstop curse of the darkness that is unwittingly perpetuated.

The situation is further complicated for minorities in that they have not only been excluded from a viable stake in the action of the present but they have also systematically been denied a sense of their past. Women's history was limited to mention of a select few women, such as Carrie Nation, Florence Nightingale, and Clara Barton; and they were prominent only because they were committed to entering the realms of male-oriented activities (war, drinking, and the like). Women such as Margaret Sanger, Amy Lowell, Mother Jones, or Nellie Bly were never mentioned, and generations were effectively raised to believe the highest occupation a woman could achieve was either a nurse or a secretary to a professional man.

Black history is a phenomenon that has seemingly just evolved with the last decade, though it was not really until the 1977 televising of Alex Haley's *Roots* that the mass population understood that Black America came from *somewhere*, had some people who did other things besides experiment with peanuts, and that proud and courageous generations of them had been pitted against a powerful and callous majority. Once again, the majority decided for the minority what it was, and the black became the reality of that impression, literally chained to that "lazy-dumb-nigger" perception, prior extensive educations notwithstanding.

The only way in which a person attracted at least partially to the same sex could understand his feelings was to try to look himself up in the abnormal psychology books under "sexual deviants." There, he read about what an outcast he was, how suicidal were his tendencies, and how maladjusted was his personality. There were no positive, open figures with whom he could identify. Growing up with shame and guilt, living in fear and in ignorance that twenty million other

Americans are at least partially of like persuasion, he eventually would evolve into an adulthood plagued with a sexual identity crisis, understandably often rendering him severely disabled.

He did not have to be this way either. Walt Whitman's poetry was edited for him in high school. From Plato to Alexander the Great to Dag Hammarskjöld, all references to same-sex love were repressed. Women never got to study their own great minds and contributions but instead were conditioned through homemaking, sewing, and typing courses. Victimized by white testing services and the denial and attempted prevention of a meaningful culture, blacks were shunted off to trade schools or no schools at all. People attracted to the same sex were relegated to the roles of weirdos, femmes, and child molesters (the latter a predominantly heterosexual disorder).

To a lesser extent and at various periods of this century, Jews, Catholics, the Irish, and Italians have been similarly victimized. Because they had an easier process of assimilation, however, these groups were able either to hide or to overcome the minority handicap and board the merry-go-round of the American dream. Once aboard as a lucky rider, empathy for those on the outside perimeter becomes seemingly less advantageous and is replaced with an "I made it, you're not trying" philosophy of misunderstood condemnation. This gets coupled to a fear that the man or woman on the perimeter will take *your* horse if given the chance to climb on and is further complicated by the notion that the only way to measure the worth of your position is by insisting on the relative lack of worth of everyone else's.

It becomes advantageous to keep everyone else off the carousel. It never occurs to the riders that if those outside see no chance of ever getting on, they will either change the rules, throw off the riders, or destroy the ride altogether—and why not?

RIGHTS MINORITIES ARE GIVEN

In fact, minorities are given just enough by the powered to retain a semblance of hope. This has the effect of making them least helpful to and in fact most vitriolic against other minorities similarly situated. They live in separate neighborhoods, send their children to separate schools, and thereby insure a total ignorance of the beauty and worth of divergent cultures and ways of thinking. Most people fear what they don't understand or what they don't know, and they grow to hate what they fear.

No one stops to see who owns the merry-go-round or the amusement park, because by design of the real owners—the powered in society—everyone is distracted by the path of the moving circle. The "average American" thus beats off fabricated minority enemies and never comprehends who is really stopping him from genuine progress. His resultant position at best remains relatively the same, though public opinion polls confirm most peoples' belief that the quality of our lives is constantly deteriorating. A second car or a color TV has done little to alter that feeling, and yet that is what keeps people in line, hoping and defending with blind hatred against false enemies.

How does all of this fit into a chapter on the practical rights of minorities? It is necessary to understand the sociological trap into which minorities allow themselves to be snared before approaching the existing laws. The basic premise of minority rights is that minorities will be granted only those rights that the majority—which is really only a phantom labeling of how the powerful want the mass of Americans to respond—wants them to have. And they will be given only the bare minimum, through laws and the promise of their enforcement and expansion, to keep them from overrunning the above-discussed carousel. Laws are retracted and repealed when they start to make for genuine progress.

Laws are passed when the majority feels threatened. The rest of the time is spent in a sense of false security, as we witnessed in the fifties and most of the seventies.

A legal treatise on minority rights is completely outdated within a few years, not because society is constantly righting its wrong, but because liberties are allowed and then denied, allowed and then denied. A defendant has certain rights under a Kennedy Court and fewer rights under a Nixon Court. Blacks may have the Civil Rights Act of 1964 interpreted broadly in the Johnson years, more narrowly in the Carter years. Miami may prohibit sexual preference discrimination one month and overturn the decision the next. Aid for cities is passed after a riot; it is withdrawn once things are quiet in the name of fiscal austerity.

LAWS PROTECTING WOMEN

Women are declared equal in 1978 and not in need of a constitutional amendment, while in most states the offenses of seduction, rape, and discrimination impose divergent standards of behavior upon females and males. Abortion may be upheld as a woman's constitutional right one year and denied the following year. Even a simple glance at the laws on prostitution illustrate that what is appropriate for one sex is punishable by the sex in power against the less powerful and necessarily submissive other sex. Because prostitutes are a powerless minority within a minority, even the larger minority of women, of which prostitutes are a part, does not consider their struggle as a part of the whole. Women as a group do not yet see the direct threat posed against them all by the unequal treatment of certain members of their own sex.

A woman may have various forms of public assistance terminated and the duty of her support transferred to any man, whether or not her actual spouse, who is found to be living in her house. No such restrictions are levied against the sexual conduct of male recipients of public assistance. Men wrote those laws because men are in full control of legislative power. And it is men who question the necessity and even mock the drive of women for proportional representation in legislatures. It is no wonder.

Minimum ages for various types of activities are different for each sex. Property laws in many states, including community property states, still greatly favor men. Psychological effects, economic hardship, and even genuine concerns as to the health of the woman have no weight in many sections of the country if a woman resident wants an abortion. Again, a woman has control of her own body only to the extent that the majority sex in power will allow her to retain it. We have had painted for us a stereotypical portrait of the woman seeking an abortion: She is a teen-ager, on drugs, very poor, and uneducated. Actually, most illegal abortions are performed upon married women with children.

We are taught to hide such facts. Their exposure would cause us to question the illusions we have been told to follow, which would destroy those who most profit by the oppression of minorities. In one form or another, each member of the alleged majority is a part of some of these minorities; and together they uphold the system that favors a very few, unconscious of how discrimination against any group is holding nearly everyone down.

The Equal Pay Act of 1963, which amended the Fair Labor Standards Act, attempted to square somewhat the problems of sex-based wage discrimination. This act requires women workers to be paid the same wage as male workers performing similar tasks. However, the Act is limited in the circumstances in which it may be applied, and many female employees are unaffected by it. Only about half of the states in the country have their own equal pay laws, and those vary individually with respect to whom they cover. The Equal Pay

Act is enforced by the Wage and Hour Division of the Department of Labor.

Women who feel their employers are not giving them equal pay for an equal job should contact a local office of the Wage and Hour Division. If there isn't one near you, you may contact the national office at the U.S. Department of Labor, and they will send you the necessary information. The important thing is to file the complaint so that action has a chance of being taken. If the woman's wages were found to be unduly less than a man's salary performing the same work, she can win all the back wages she should have earned within two years of the complaint, plus additional money for legal fees and her attorney's fees. In certain instances where willful discrimination is proven, even more money can be awarded.

The Equal Pay Act covers only wage discrimination. As it does not protect women against the vices of preferential job assignments, job transfers, and the like, it is of a fairly limited scope. These other problems are in part covered by Title VII, administered by the Equal Employment Opportunities Commission and discussed hereafter. Both the Equal Pay Act and Title VII of the Civil Rights Act of 1964 may be invoked to combat suspected discrimination. The Labor Department seems to move a bit quicker than the EEOC, however, because of its less-backlogged agenda and more limited scope of enforcement. All employers are covered under the Equal Pay Act, be they administrative, executive, or professional companies or individuals.

Title VII: Rights for Women
Under the Civil Rights Act of 1964, some more substantial barriers were lifted against women by establishment of a potential for penalizing employers who unreasonably refused to hire women for jobs they were able to perform. The now famous Title VII of the Civil Rights Act designated sex discrimination as an unlawful employment practice in both

labor organizations and among employers. Remedies provided for in the act for aggrieved parties included money, damages, and injunctive relief.

It should be noted that this law probably would not have been passed except for its camouflage amid legislation curbing racial and ethnic discrimination. But the majority was at this time willing to grant minorities, most notably black Americans, these rights. The women's section of the law was a relatively hidden prize in the box.

The development of sex discrimination interpretations of Title VII has been fairly brisk. The EEOC has developed a significant body of administrative regulations that admittedly have resulted in some changes in American life. One need not go back very far to remember how strange it was to see a female bus driver or hear the voice of a male telephone operator or airline steward.

Title VII covers employers in businesses and industries affecting commerce as well as labor organizations involved in these and related industries. The act is constructed to permit the EEOC to attempt conciliation of employment disputes. Accordingly, there are certain time limits which the commission must be allowed in an attempt to gain voluntary compliance with Title VII before private lawsuits may be brought. The investigation by the Commission may lead to intervention in an aggrieved person's private suit or may otherwise be used by the government to redress the wrong.

Title VII does not offer protection to employees working for companies with less than fifteen employees, although employees of small companies may still have recourse with local or state employment laws.

The procedures for filing a complaint under Title VII can be very complex. The law requires that any individual who files a charge with the Equal Employment Opportunities Commission must initially file the complaint with an appropriate state agency. Your local office of the EEOC will tell you the name of that state agency, but failure to file in both places may later preclude a recovery for damages or lost wages.

Many EEOC offices are overworked, while others are unresponsive and inefficient. Title VII provides that any individual aggrieved by employment practices of his employer who has filed with the EEOC may bring a private lawsuit if the Commission has not satisfactorily acted within a half a year of having been advised of that complaint.

As the EEOC is the Federal agency that administers Title VII, and as Title VII is the broadest protection so far given to aggrieved minorities in their battle against discrimination, every person so aggrieved should utilize the powers of that Commission. A complaint is begun at an EEOC office by the complainant filling out a "charge form." This form is so designated because, in effect, the employer is being charged with discriminatory practices.

The EEOC does not have the power to force the employer to desist from his discrimination; it can only attempt to get him to stop through conciliation. If the Commission does not succeed, the complainant then has the right to pursue the matter in court. Direct pursual in the courts is not permitted prior to an attempt to conciliate through the available administrative channels.

As there is often a backlog of a couple of years on these complaints with the EEOC, the exhaustion of administrative remedies can be exhausting and discouraging for an aggrieved party interested in justice. Nonetheless, use of Title VII offers the best chance of achieving an effective resolution of matters pertaining to discrimination.

Executive Orders for Women's Rights

Executive Orders from the Oval Office have provided women with additional ammunition in the battle against bigotry. Executive Order No. 11478 requires that Federal agencies and departments cannot discriminate and must establish affirmative action programs to involve women more equitably in significant positions within the Federal bureaucracy. Executive Order No. 11246, as amended by Executive Order No. 11375, says that any employer who has a contract with the Federal government cannot discriminate on the grounds of gender. This order is enforced by the Office of Federal Contract Compliance within the Department of Labor.

State Laws for Women's Rights

Most states have also passed laws prohibiting discrimination in employment on the basis of sex. The states have their own equal pay acts, fair employment practice acts, and the like, largely based upon their Federal counterparts just discussed. The states have established commissions against discrimination, known by various names, that have jurisdiction over claims of job prejudice within the state; they are analogous to what the EEOC can do on a national level. These state commissions are good sources for information on how to best proceed with a case; they are also often a legal forum that can award monetary and injunctive relief.

THE FOURTEENTH AMENDMENT

The key doctrine utilized to combat discrimination is the Fourteenth Amendment to the Constitution. It states that "no state shall . . . deny to any person within its jurisdiction the equal protection of the laws." Used to combat decades of discrimination, this amendment has served as the key to unlock the entrenched discriminatory laws and practices of the majority. Discrimination was actually law, because it protected the wealth of the powered in society. Not only did the powered whites pass laws against the minority blacks, but the white legislatures denied voting rights to blacks, as well as to women, so that neither could until very recently ever gain any form of meaningful power. There is still no parity.

Segregated schools and segregated public accommodations were the law until twenty-five years ago and are still fact throughout most of the country today. Voting districts and school districts are gerrymandered today in patterns that exclude meaningful black representation from black and even mixed neighborhoods. It is done legally, voted on by legislatures and signed by governors, and it is designed to keep power where it is. Banks still "redline" (or approve mortgages for minorities only within certain defined geographical neighborhoods), thereby creating and perpetuating segregated neighborhoods and ghettoes.

Hence, while a compliance with the Equal Protection Clause should prohibit a state from denying any person the protection of equal laws, the state manages in the name of its unrepresentative laws to treat its citizens differently. Banks view their investments in city property as threatened by the incursion of minorities, and so they keep people locked up in defined sections away from their investments.

Equal protection supposedly compels the courts to declare invalid those laws which favor one group over another in violation of the principle of equal treatment otherwise compelled by the Fourteenth Amendment. However, the standards the courts apply in 1977 are different from 1970 and will be different in 1980. Equal protection is a matter of degree and is decided overwhelmingly by white males influenced by the circumstances of the moment. This is why denying benefits for pregnancy may be constitutional while allowing benefits for baldness treatments is perfectly legitimate. Where the powered are benefited, their laws will bear them out: The alleged institutions of the majority only serve to legitimize these decisions.

Reasonable discrimination, where it is logical for one reason or another to place people in different categories, does not violate the Equal Protection Clause. However, it may be alleged to be reasonable for a state to prohibit women from holding jobs as bartenders because of the increased social and moral problems created by women in bars. That court finding, like so many others in the second half of the twentieth century, gives states the ability to legitimately discriminate, constitutional proscriptions notwithstanding.

In recent years, the courts are applying a strict scrutiny test to sex-classification cases. However, openly professed homosexual teachers are considered unworthy of protection against firing, on the specious grounds that they are anxious to recruit converts among young children. (Sometimes singer Anita Bryant used such hysteria tactics in 1977 to whip up sentiments against a Dade County, Florida, ordinance that prohibited discrimination against people with same-sex preferences. She ignored the reality that most child molesters are heterosexual and most victims are females, often related to the offender.)

Equal protection in truth only applies to some groups. Remember that the Vietnam War protesters were arrested in the 1960s despite constitutional amendments and case law procluding any abridgement of free speech. The Constitution as applied to those without power is far more of a tool of the times than a guide through all times. The final Attorney General Mitchell-ordered round-up in Washington involving mass arrests and the mass Clamshell Alliance arrests at a New Hampshire nuclear plant protest perhaps best illustrate the verity of this observation.

The Fourteenth Amendment (like the Equal Rights Amendment) prohibits only discrimination by Federal, state, and local governments. These governments are not allowed either to engage in discriminatory practices or to legislate laws that discriminate. Its effect is limited to actions in which the government or one of its institutions is involved, although certain private institutions that perform functions normally thought of as governmental or private activity supported by public funds may also be affected by the Fourteenth Amendment.

OTHER MINORITY PROTECTION

State Agencies

The various state agencies referred to in the discussion on women's rights also have jurisdiction in cases involving discrimination on the basis of race, religion, or national origin. The state proceedings are usually quicker than Federal forums and some results satisfactory to the complainant can be achieved. In fact, under Title VII, proceedings will be deferred to state agencies for action for a period of two months before the EEOC can act.

Even if the EEOC determines that there is no basis for the aggrieved party's charge and the relevant state agency or attorney general's office has not effectively settled or prosecuted the action, the complaining party can institute a private suit on his own initiative against the offender. However the suit is brought, it must be shown that the employee was classified or treated adversely because of his race, religion, color, sex, or national origin. Charges must have been filed before the EEOC within 90 days after the unlawful practice or within 210 days after the occurrence when a local procedure has been utilized.

Sections 1981 and 1983 Protections

The right to be free from discharge from employment because of race or color is also protected under part of the United States Code. Sections 1981 and 1983 provide civil remedies for anyone subjected to the deprivation of any civil right secured by the U.S. Constitution if the acts were deemed to be under the "color of law," as long as some state action was involved in the action.

In order to maintain an action under 1983, it is not necessary to allege or prove that the offender intended to deprive the victim of his constitutional rights or that he acted with purposeful intent. It is sufficient merely to establish that the deprivation of constitutional rights or privileges was the natural consequence of the actions of the offender acting under color of law, irrespective of whether such consequence was intended. Actual proof that the offender was motivated by racial prejudice is not necessarily required, only a showing of discrimination.

If you suspect discrimination in housing or employment on the grounds of race or sex, contact your state agency in charge of hearing such cases. Also contact the local or national offices of the EEOC or, where relevant, the Department of Labor. In the instance of housing discrimination, HUD is the proper agency to contact. Only by the full and conscientious use of what laws do exist can a small dent be made in the steel wall that still blocks us from genuine progress.

MINORITY RIGHTS IN REALITY TODAY

Until the last decade, most black Americans were in the lower economic class in this country. They were denied entry into meaningful jobs, prevented from joining unions and paid far less for the same job performed by whites, when they were able to get such jobs. Denied access and mortgage financing into most decent neighborhoods, they were ghettoized, where only irregular and rudimentary city services were provided. Black schools were intentionally made inferior by all-white school committees, thereby insuring the next generation of trapped, uneducated citizens. Public housing with thousands of units—on a minimum of land—literally have bred a new generation of hardened, bitter people.

Not that much has changed. Despite Fair Housing Laws, many realtors still show homes according to the skin color of the prospective purchaser. Government jobs and education have opened up somewhat, but the feeling in the late 1970s seems to be exemplified by whites declaring blacks should not be given special treatment over them in college admission, as though blacks had been given an equal shake in grammar school, in high school, on college boards, or in their study environments. The courts of the late 1970s in effect seem to be returning to a slightly convoluted version of "separate but equal" under the color of law.

Once again there are laws on the books that attempt to portray a semblance of progress, but they are laws that were passed only to assuage, to fashion a "here and there" type of progress, and do little to give minorities rights commensurate with the majority's. The way in which a law is applied is of far greater import than the law itself. It can be like having a new car in the driveway that no one knows how to drive.

As of this writing, people who are attracted to the same sex enjoy no such protection. For some reason, legislators and judges overwhelmingly feel that these people, numbering in the tens of millions in the United States alone, are not entitled to normal protection in housing or employment because of their sexual preference. Ancient and misquoted passages from the Bible, usually discredited by modern society, are quoted by self-espoused savers of children as the Gospel justification for condemning people in every facet of life. Although this is hardly a Christian or legally equal treatment, it is working for this generation the way McCarthyism and the Dixiecrats worked in the past.

Currently, thirty cities and four counties have banned discrimination based upon "affectional or sexual preference." A number of these communities are college towns, which tend to be more liberal in their approach to guaranteeing every citizen his right to pursue his own life as long as it does not interfere with the rights of others.

Another thirteen cities, including San Francisco, New York City, and Boston, have enacted some form of equal employment provisions for homosexuals. Columbus, Ohio, has passed an antidiscrimination law for public accommodations and housing.

Nineteen states have repealed their sex laws to eliminate

the "crime against nature," widely referred to as the sodomy statutes.

Across the nation, courts are beginning to grant all people the right to privacy. The Massachusetts Supreme Court recently declared in the *Balthazar* case that private acts between consenting adults cannot be regulated. The U.S. District Court for California declared that the Navy cannot discharge a serviceperson merely because of his or her sexual affection without evaluating the person's fitness to serve in the light of all relevant factors. *Saal* v. *Middendorf* stands for the proposition that discharge cannot be mandatory merely because of a same-sex preference.

The courts have also found in a number of jurisdictions that universities must recognize homophile groups on campus. Recognition has been awarded on the basis of the equal protection clause and the First Amendment clauses of the Constitution.

In Washington, D. C., the City Council passed a bill protecting gay parents seeking custody or visitation rights. The law states that sexual orientation cannot be a conclusive consideration in and of itself in child custody cases. A growing number of family court and probate court judges are awarding visitation rights to gay parents, though custody victories are still relatively rare.

Local Commissions Against Discrimination generally do not recognize affectional preferences as the basis for protection against discrimination. For example, the Civil Rights Commission of the state of Michigan denies any authority even to investigate complaints of discrimination due not only to homosexuality but also a physical or mental handicap. They deny that freedom from discrimination is a basic civil right.

Even the United States Government's Immigration and Naturalization Service has announced a major turnabout in its position on the naturalization of people who engage in sex with others of the same gender. INS's lawyer stated recently that "The fact that a petitioner for naturalization is or has been a practicing homosexual during the relevant statutory period is not, in itself, a sufficient basis for finding that he lacks the necessary good moral character." The INS has long been one of the most arbitrarily narrow government agencies in the realm of minority rights.

In late 1973 the American Psychiatric Association by unanimous vote ruled that homosexuality "should no longer be listed as 'mental disorder'" in its official nomenclature of mental disorders and urged that homosexuals be given all the protections guaranteed to other citizens. They state that sexual preference should have no correlation with a person's right to housing and a job.

The APA was not, of course, implying that all "homosexuals" are healthy. Given the denial to them of an equal stake in society, this would be an unlikely premise. Those who are disturbed by, in conflict with, or who wish to change their sexual orientation are now deemed to have a sexual orientation disturbance. No one is advocating taking off the books legislation aimed at regulating child molesters, rapists, assaulters, or those who attempt sex unwarranted by the other party. Full protection against these crimes, equally committed by members of every sexual and personal persuasion, is still in effect in every jurisdiction in the country.

What the APA and the law reformers are attempting to bring to the fore is that same-sex preference in and of itself implies no impairment in judgment, stability, or rehabilitative or vocational capabilities; and it therefore makes no sense to deny perfectly healthy good citizens their due rights to the necessities of life such as a home and a job. Denying these basics of life has the same deleterious effect as denying blacks good educations and a choice of homes. It is the same as denying women the right to a day's pay for the day's work of their choice. Ultimately, society will have to pay the price for disabling a viable though divergent part of its whole being.

Only when the mass of American citizens comes to see that each of us belongs to several minorities that together constitute a majority will all of us enjoy the quality of life that has deluded us by our own self-denial. In the meantime, there are laws that can have some meaning and can make for small steps of progress if used conscientiously and with a dedication of purpose. However, without basic realizations and realignments in the thinking of our people, the rights of minorities will continue to be in the stranglehold of a select few. They continue to succeed in manipulating good people into thinking they are serving some illusory majority that should have but never has improved the society in which each one of us is a minority of one.

9

Criminal Law And the Criminal Process

Though there are many analogies between criminal law and some areas of civil law, there are many features unique to the practice of criminal law. "Crimes" are acts that society, through its legislative bodies and its courts, chooses to forbid and punish. Because we in the United States sanctify the value of individual liberty and because the sanctions of criminal law usually involve the potential removal of that liberty, our lawmakers have made criminal law into an exceptionally technical and complex area of law. Within the legal profession, criminal law is increasingly becoming a specialized field.

Crimes are considered offenses against the citizenry—either the citizenry of the entire nation or the citizenry of the particular state where the crime takes place. The Attorney General of the United States, with the FBI and the regional U.S. Attorney offices, prosecutes federal crimes. These include all routine crimes in federal enclaves such as the District of Columbia. In addition, congressional statutes have created specific federal crimes of general, nationwide application. Usually Congress defines such a federal interest only for an act that is more than local in scope, such as interstate and international smuggling, income-tax evasion, or the robbery of a bank insured by the federal government.

Such cases are entitled "The United States of America against Jane Doe," and they are brought in a U.S. District Court. The definitions of the crimes and the procedures to be used in the federal courts are derived from the U.S. Constitution, the laws passed by Congress, and the mandates of the federal courts. These courts, by publishing opinions explaining their decisions in individual cases, are lawmakers; and they have an enormous impact upon the constantly evolving area of criminal law. Because it has the final say in interpreting the U.S. Constitution, the U.S. Supreme Court plays a particularly important role in making criminal law.

The overwhelming majority of crimes are defined and prosecuted at the state and local level. These cases have titles such as "The State against Jane Doe," "The People of the State of *Kankan* against Jane Doe," or "The Commonwealth of *New Omin* against Jane Doe." These cases are investigated by state and local police agencies; they are prosecuted by the state's Attorney General or, most frequently, by a local district attorney or county prosecutor. These crimes, and the procedures to be used in prosecuting them, are defined primarily by the state legislatures and the opinions of state appellate courts. However, particularly in the last two decades, the U.S. Supreme Court has held that more and more of the provisions of the U.S. Constitution, as interpreted by them, are binding upon the states.

Each of the jurisdictions that prosecutes crimes is independent of the others. For this reason, the definitions of various crimes and the procedures used to prosecute them vary among the states and the federal government. However, because of our shared historical and legal roots, together with the portions of the U.S. Constitution that have been deemed to have nationwide impact, there are many common features to the criminal law in these various jurisdictions.

CRIMINALS AND CRIMES

Parties to a Crime

One need not pull the trigger, hold the gun, or even be present at the shooting to be found criminally liable. For example, the getaway driver who sits outside in a car is considered a principal in a robbery, just as guilty as those who go into the bank with guns. If one is at or near the scene of the crime, participates in some way, and shares the intent necessary to be considered guilty, then one is guilty under the theory of "joint enterprise."

One may also be guilty of an attempted crime though the crime itself never took place. To be guilty of an attempted crime, one must generally commit some overt act (which can be very slight), and one must demonstrate an intent that the crime take place. In an attempt, the crime itself has usually been prevented only by some unforeseen circumstance, such as the arrival of the police, rather than simply a change of heart on the part of the perpetrator. Merely intending to commit a crime or merely preparing to commit a crime generally will not be sufficient actions to constitute an attempt. The penalties for attempts usually vary in proportion to (and are less than) the penalties for the completed crimes.

Similarly, one may be guilty of a *conspiracy* to commit a crime, whether or not the crime actually takes place. Conspiracy usually consists of a combination, with some acts or words signifying an agreement, between two or more persons to commit some crime. In many jurisdictions, to be a conspirator one must commit some overt act (however slight) in furtherance of the conspiracy. Co-conspirators, like the members of a joint enterprise, are usually responsible for all the crimes committed by the other co-conspirators, as long as the crimes are not beyond the scope of the conspiracy. Thus, one bank robber may be guilty of the shooting of a guard by another co-conspirator if it takes place during, and in furtherance of, a robbery. Unlike an attempt, conspiracy is an independent crime; one can be charged with both conspiracy and the crime itself. As with an attempt, the punishments for conspiracies vary in proportion to the punishments for the intended crimes.

Somebody who assists in the preparation for a crime, such as buying the guns, but who does not assist at the scene of the actual crime is an accessory before the fact if the crime is committed. Usually an accessory before the fact can be punished the same as a principal.

If somebody knows that a crime has been committed and voluntarily assists one of the principal criminals in an effort to prevent the arrest of the principal, then the person giving such assistance is an accessory after the fact, unless the principal is a close relative. An accessory after the fact is also punished in proportion to the principal's offense.

Mental Capacity

Our legal system recognizes that, under some circumstances, a person should not be held responsible for certain acts that would otherwise be considered criminal. Thus, a person who is put in a state of fear and forced to commit a crime is excused from criminal liability because it would be unfair to punish someone for involuntary behavior. Another example would be acts committed during an epileptic seizure.

Similarly, most crimes encompass a requirement that a certain mental element, or intent, be proven along with the prohibited act. Often the criminal must be shown to have *intended* a certain result; but some crimes are defined with other mental states, such as malicious, knowing, reckless, or negligent behavior.

Thus, if one is mistaken about an underlying fact, the criminal intent may be lacking; for example, one would not (in most states) be guilty of bigamy if one honestly believed one's first spouse had died.

In limited areas, mostly concerning public health, safety, and morality, courts allow legislatures to impose *strict liability*, under which standard there is no requirement of proof of any mental state. For example, statutory rape is not excused by an honest, mistaken belief that the girl was of legal age. Such a law is obviously harsh, and it represents the exception rather than the rule.

A person is also excused from criminal responsibility if he was mentally ill at the time he committed an otherwise criminal act and if, as a result of that illness, he was unable either to realize that the act was wrong or to control his behavior. This is the "insanity defense"; such a person is found "not guilty by reason of temporary insanity." Generally speaking, such a person is institutionalized at a state mental hospital, many of which are no better than prisons.

If a person is mentally ill to such an extent that he is incapable of understanding the criminal proceedings and assisting his counsel, then the person is usually hospitalized indefinitely until he is competent to stand trial.

Addiction to alcohol or narcotics is not in itself punishable, as it is considered a status, not an act. However, such addiction is not treated the same as is an epileptic fit or a mental illness, because our legal system continues to view the ingestion of such drugs as "voluntary" and, therefore, insufficient to excuse other criminal acts, such as possession of narcotics or burglary. Generally speaking, drug use is pertinent only in mitigation of the punishment. However, if a person is under the influence of a drug at the time he commits an act, he may occasionally be found to be lacking the specific intent necessary to be considered criminally liable.

Finally, our legal system puts young people in a special category. In most jurisdictions, a youth under a certain age, such as age seven, is considered incapable of any legal responsibility for otherwise criminal acts. Between that lower limit and an upper limit of about sixteen or seventeen, a youth may be found responsible if he knew the nature of the act and knew right from wrong. But he is not found "criminal"; he is called instead a "juvenile delinquent."

Our system presumes that delinquent children should, if possible, remain with their families and be rehabilitated, rather than put in prisons. When juveniles are incarcerated, it is often in facilities where the emphasis, at least in theory, is on education and rehabilitation.

The pendulum, though, is swinging back in favor of harsher treatment of juvenile delinquents. Many jurisdictions have procedures permitting juveniles above a certain age, such as twelve or fourteen, to be treated as adult criminals if their crimes are exceptionally serious or if their records demonstrate repeated brushes with the law.

Felonies and Misdemeanors

Most crimes fall into one of two categories, felonies or misdemeanors, depending on the potential punishment. *Felonies* are all crimes punishable by death or incarceration in state prison, which usually means a maximum possible sentence of more than one year. *Misdemeanors* are less serious offenses punishable only by incarceration in local or county jails, usually for a maximum period of one year. In some places, for some offenses, a previous conviction can change a misdemeanor into a felony. Some jurisdictions have a third category of minor "offenses," such as public drunkenness.

In most jurisdictions these distinctions have various practical effects at different steps of the criminal process, such as the right to arrest someone without a warrant, the method by which one is formally charged with a crime, and maybe the size of the jury for a trial. Though there has been a recent trend to forgive, forget, and revoke such laws, in many jurisdictions a conviction for a felony still may entail loss of certain privileges such as the rights to vote, hold public office, or acquire certain licenses or permits.

Crimes against the Person

Homicide is the killing of another human being; some homicides are excusable and others are crimes, usually felonies. *Murder* is a killing with "malice aforethought," which means an intentional killing.

The necessary intent need only be an intention to cause great bodily harm or else actions (such as causing an airplane accident) taken with the knowledge that someone's death will probably result. Murder is in the second degree unless there is a showing of deliberation and premeditation, in which case it is first-degree murder. No minimum time period or amount of planning is necessary to constitute deliberation and premeditation.

In some jurisdictions there is a *felony-murder* rule stating that any killing that takes place during the course of any felony will constitute murder. Under some circumstances, such as a killing during the commission of a felony punishable by life imprisonment, it may be ranked as murder in the first degree. Some view this rule as excessively harsh, especially since it applies to an accomplice, who may not contemplate any violence but may be convicted of murder under the joint enterprise theory. First-degree murder has a more severe penalty than second-degree murder, such as the death penalty or life imprisonment with no parole.

A killing that takes place unjustifiably but in the heat of passion or under provocation is considered unintentional and, therefore, is defined as the less serious offense of *manslaughter*. For example, a killing resulting from excessive use of force during mutual combat or a heated argument would be manslaughter. In addition, grossly reckless behavior, such as driving a car while under the influence of a strong dosage of drugs or narcotics, may constitute manslaughter if someone's death results. Manslaughter in some places may be in the first or second degree, with punishment varying accordingly, depending on whether or not a dangerous weapon was used.

In some jurisdictions, there is a category of *negligent homicide* for a killing that results from the failure to exercise reasonable caution. Negligent homicide is less serious than manslaughter, and it may even be a misdemeanor.

There are many other crimes against the person. *Kidnapping* is the forcible confining or taking of a person against his will. If done with an intention to extort a ransom, it is usually an aggravated form of kidnapping, and the penalty may be death or life imprisonment.

Robbery is the stealing of somebody's property by using force against the person with custody of the property or by threatening that person and putting him in fear. If a weapon is shown or used (or, in some jurisdictions, merely threatened), it is an armed robbery, and the penalty may be greater.

Assault and battery is an unjustified and intentional touching of another person with an intent to injure that person. An assault is simply an attempted assault and battery or a threat of an imminent assault and battery which puts someone in immediate and reasonable fear. Simple assault or simple assault and battery are usually misdemeanors.

There are numerous kinds of *aggravated assaults*, most of which are felonies. Some of them are aggravated by an additional element of intent, such as assault with intent to murder, rape, or rob. Others are aggravated by the use of a dangerous weapon, such as assault by means of a dangerous weapon or assault and battery by means of a dangerous weapon. Anything that could cause serious injury, no matter how many everyday uses it may have, can be considered a dangerous weapon in the particular circumstances of a given case.

Rape is unlawful intercourse with a person by force or fear and against the person's will, that is, without consent.

Rape laws have traditionally been applied exclusively to female victims, but some jurisdictions have recently expanded these laws to protect male victims as well. The potential punishment for rape is often life imprisonment or, in some places, death. Largely because of public pressure by women's rights spokespersons in the last five years, rapists are now more frequently convicted and more frequently sentenced to long prison terms.

Other areas of sexual behavior have traditionally been considered criminal regardless of the consent of the parties. These laws, with archaic titles such as "sodomy," "the infamous crime against nature," or "unnatural and lascivious acts," historically have been prohibited on such specious rationales as that they "violate the natural order of the divine universe" and "undermine the moral fiber of society." Civil libertarians, including some judges and state legislatures, have recently ruled that the state has no business questioning the behavior of consenting adults in the privacy of their own bedrooms. (See the Minority Rights chapter.)

Several common defenses can be raised to justify or excuse an act that would otherwise constitute a crime against the person. The consent of the so-called victim is usually a defense to rape, kidnapping, and the various forms of assault. However, there is no excuse if the force applied is beyond the scope of the consent given, as for a shooting during a football pile-up. The law allows the use of a reasonable amount of force to effect an arrest of a person reasonably believed to have committed a felony.

Finally, force is justified by self-defense if a person uses no more force than necessary to protect his own life and limb. Some jurisdictions allow the use of a reasonable force to protect one's property or to defend a third person's life and limb. Whether or not the force used was reasonable is a question to be determined ultimately by a jury or other factfinder.

Crimes Against Property

The most fundamental property crime is *larceny*, the technical word for "stealing," which refers to the unlawful taking of somebody else's property with the intention to permanently deprive that person of possession of the property. If force or fear upon the victim is the means of the taking, then it becomes a robbery; if the victim is unaware of the theft, such as by a pickpocket, it is at most an aggravated larceny, called larceny from the person.

Most jurisdictions have distinctions of degree between *grand larceny* and *petty larceny*, usually according to the value of the property stolen, with the former often being a felony and the latter a misdemeanor. Many shoplifting offenses are petty larcenies, as the cut-off value may be as much as $100. Most larceny statutes now encompass all kinds of taking, including embezzlement, larceny by false pretenses, and so on.

Receiving, or possessing, *stolen property* is a crime if the possessor knows that the property is stolen. This knowledge can be inferred from the circumstances, such as the fact that the property was recently stolen. Again, the punishment may vary according to the value of the property.

There are numerous crimes associated with *forgery* of various legal and financial documents or with the uttering (attempting to pass or cash) of such a forged instrument. These crimes usually require a showing that the forger or utterer knew the instrument was forged and intended to defraud somebody. It should be noted that writing a check that the maker knows will bounce or be stopped by you or the bank may be enough to sustain a criminal act of fraud against him.

Numerous statutes cover malicious or intentional injury to someone's property. *Arson* is the burning of a building with a willful or malicious mental state. If an intention to defraud an insurance company can be proven, it may be an aggravated form of arson, with a heavier penalty.

Burglary is a breaking and entering into a building with an intention to commit another crime. The intention, again, is usually inferred from the entry. Most jurisdictions have various degrees of burglary, depending on whether several factors are also present—the most serious being one where the perpetrator is armed, enters a dwelling at night, and actually assaults a person lawfully present. In most states it is a crime to possess a burglar's tool, one designed to break into a building or depository, if there is an inference that a person intended so to use it and to commit a felony.

Crimes against property are usually considered somewhat less serious than crimes involving personal violence. In urban areas, especially the first time someone is convicted, punishment for property crimes is often mitigated by the social or economic deprivation of the perpetrator.

Miscellaneous Crimes

Not only are there many other crimes against the person and crimes against property, but there are also many crimes that are more difficult to categorize. Among these are certain offenses against the judicial system itself, such as *perjury*, which is willfully and knowingly making a false statement under oath with a corrupt intent.

Numerous criminal offenses involve an effort to bolster and protect the "morals" of society, often by punishing consensual behavior in *victimless* crimes. Sexual activity has been discussed, but also in this category are laws forbidding obscene publications and movies, gambling, and prostitution. Though these activities may conceivably sometimes (and the evidence is certainly unclear on this) have a harmful effect on the participants, it is difficult to justify imposing criminal sanctions on adult people who are their own "victims" and who willingly run whatever risks are involved.

In addition, law enforcement in these widely practiced areas is extremely uneven, thereby giving the opportunity for the appearance of discriminatory enforcement, hypocritical punishment, and corruption. Such crimes create disrespect for the law among otherwise law-abiding citizens, who see no rationale for the criminal stigma attached to apparently harmless, commonplace activities.

Some of these morality offenses tread extremely close to recognized areas of constitutionally protected liberties. Obscenity, for example, is very hard to distinguish from protected freedoms of speech, press, and privacy. After decades of seemingly endless litigation, the U.S. Supreme Court has developed a definition of obscenity that continues to spawn a barrage of legal challenges. The current requirements for a judgment of *obscenity* are that the material, when judged by "the average person" applying contemporary and local community standards, appeal predominently to a prurient interest in sexual matters, portray sexual conduct in a patently offensive way, and not have serious literary, artistic, political, or scientific value. The publishers, theater-owners, enforcement agencies, and courts have found this definition to be as confusing as it seems. Under our Constitution, in theory, criminal laws are not supposed to be vague and confusing.

Finally, there are many items and substances which the law declares to be contraband and illegal to possess or distribute. Some of these items, such as weapons of various sorts, have no potential use other than to harm another person. The laws vary on many of these items; and one must be careful in travelling from one state to another with some items, such as firearms. Ironically, though, some of the harmful weapons are less regulated than some of the substances whose harmfulness is less clear.

Most states have criminal laws forbidding the possession and use of many drugs, excluding alcohol; distribution, sale, and possession with intent to distribute such drugs is a more serious crime, usually a felony. Some of these drugs, primarily heroin and other morphine derivatives, are physically addictive and can cause severe disruption to the personal life of the addict. Such drugs clearly demand some form of public regulation and, probably, a prohibition against unregulated distribution. However, the criminalization of these items is considered by many to be not only ineffective but also counterproductive, because it creates a black market with erratic quality and high prices. The prices, in turn, cause some users of these drugs to commit property crimes in order to obtain money for drugs. For this reason, some experts believe we should try the approach used in England, where narcotics are dispensed openly and only by government agencies.

Some liberalization of marijuana laws has taken place in a few jurisdictions, which have recently decriminalized the personal use and possession of marijuana. These states have recognized that the results have been similar to Prohibition, when criminal sanctions were applied to a widely practiced, victimless activity.

Finally, a word about the defense of *entrapment*, which is often raised (but not often successfully) in the offenses dealing with health, welfare, and morals. If law enforcement officers instigate a crime by implanting a criminal idea in an innocent mind and thereby bring about a crime that otherwise would never have been committed, the defendants have the defense of entrapment available to excuse them from criminal liability. In most instances, however, the prosecution can successfully show that the defendants had the disposition to commit the crime and the undercover police only provided the opportunity for its perpetration. This predisposition usually dissolves the defense of entrapment.

THE PRE-TRIAL PROCESS

Investigation and Arrest

Once a crime is committed, or simply reported, the labyrinth of the criminal law process begins to unfold. Law enforcement agencies generally cannot compel information, except through a grand jury. Instead, they must rely upon citizen cooperation, informers motivated by malevolence or monetary reward, the belief by many (usually mistaken) that there exists some obligation to cooperate with the police, and fear of reprisals or detention (which would often be illegal). If they possess enough information to obtain one, a search warrant is another tool available to them.

Assuming that finger-pointing information is obtained, each jurisdiction has its own definition of what constitutes legal grounds to bring a person into the criminal justice system. Most frequently this is done by means of an *arrest*, which is physically taking the suspect into custody. According to the U.S. Supreme Court, the preferred way of making an arrest is by means of an *arrest warrant*, which is a written order, issued by a judicial officer (judge, magistrate, or justice of the peace), directing the law enforcement officers to arrest and bring before the court a named person charged with a crime. The warrant, like a search warrant, is obtained by taking an oath and presenting to the judicial officer *probable cause* (a reasonable ground to believe) that a crime has been committed by the suspect.

Police officers can generally arrest without a warrant any person if they have probable cause to believe that the person has committed a felony. The felony need not have been committed in the presence of the officer, and hearsay information (from third persons) or the collective knowledge of the police force may furnish the probable cause. An officer may arrest someone without a warrant if he knows that a warrant for the person's arrest has been issued and is still in effect.

For misdemeanors, the general power of police officers to make an arrest is more limited. The traditional rule has been that a misdemeanor arrest can be made only if the offense is committed in the officer's presence; in many places, it must also involve a "breach of the peace" and be continuing at the time of the arrest. Because of the obvious limitations of this rule, most jurisdictions have enacted statutory expansions of the power to arrest for misdemeanors such as shoplifting or operating a vehicle under the influence of alcohol.

Private persons generally have no authority to arrest someone for a misdemeanor. However, there are, in many places, some statutory arrest powers, such as the authority of a store employee to detain somebody seen shoplifting. For a felony, a private citizen usually has a power to arrest which is more limited than the power of a police officer. For example, in many jurisdictions, a citizen can make a legal arrest only if someone has, in fact, committed a felony; probable cause is not enough to justify the arrest.

If an arrest is justified, reasonable force is permitted to effectuate the arrest. The amount of force which will be considered legal is proportionate to the seriousness of the crime, the use of force, and the weapons possessed by the suspect. Most jurisdictions also say that a person, or at least a police officer, who has the right to make an arrest also has the right to enter a dwelling and, if necessary, break open the doors in order to make the arrest.

Police are limited in their political and geographic jurisdiction. However, they do have authority to cross over into adjoining jurisdictions in "hot pursuit" of a felony suspect and make the arrest. Between adjoining cities, towns, or counties the officer can usually bring the suspect back to the jurisdiction where the offense took place. If the pursuit is into an adjacent state, then the suspect is placed in a local jail in the state where the arrest takes place. A local judge or magistrate must determine whether the arrest is lawful. If it is, then the suspect is held to await the proceedings known as interstate rendition.

Interstate rendition is based on a provision of the U.S. Constitution (Article 4, Section 2), which mandates that "a person charged in any state with treason, felony, or other crime, who shall flee from justice and be found in another state, shall on demand of the executive authority of the state from which he fled, be delivered up . . . (to the demanding state)." Most states have enacted the model rendition law establishing uniform rendition procedures by which the governor of the demanding state can request that the governor of the asylum state turn over the "fugitive from justice," who is usually in custody in the asylum state. These procedures are usually quite routine; and the fugitive is permitted to question only the technical adequacy of the paperwork and the issue of identity (whether he is the person named in the demand). The asylum state will not listen to a claim that the charges in the demanding state are groundless. The same procedures are used for a fugitive who jumped bail or escaped from prison in the demanding state.

Between nations, the analogous procedure is called *extradition* and is governed by treaty obligations between the two nations. The U.S. has an extradition treaty with most other governments, but the categories of extraditable offenses vary. For example, extradition of draft deserters from the U.S. Army was not honored by many foreign governments during the Vietnam War.

Especially for misdemeanors and minor offenses, the alternative to an arrest is to issue a *summons* ordering the defendant into court. If the person fails to appear at court on the designated date, the court may issue an arrest warrant for the person.

The rules governing the legality of arrests are often violated; in particular, people are often arrested on mere suspicion rather than probable cause. However, the remedies for illegal arrest are pragmatically too little and too late; the illegality of the arrest is usually not grounds to get the charges dropped. A civil (tort) suit for damages is one alternative; but this is usually slow, tedious, and fruitless. If one pleads not guilty to the criminal charge and has a trial, any evidence, whether a confession or an item seized from the defendant, that was obtained as a result of an illegal arrest may be excluded from the trial, if the judge can be persuaded that the arrest was illegal. This remedy is, however, valueless to the overwhelming majority of defendants, who eventually plead guilty.

Initiation of Formal Prosecution

Formal, written criminal charges are either complaints, informations, or indictments. Complaints are made and sworn to before a judicial officer, informations are issued by prosecutors, and indictments are issued by grand juries.

The *grand jury* is a group of about twenty to thirty citizens, who usually serve for a month or more. They deliberate and act in secret, under the direction of the local prosecutor, to investigate crimes and to issue indictments. The grand jury can *subpoena* (command) witnesses to come before it, testify, and bring documents, books, and other evidence. Defense lawyers generally are not permitted in grand jury rooms, even to represent witnesses.

In addition, if a majority of grand jurors agrees that there is reason to believe a person is guilty of a crime, the grand jury issues an *indictment*. In theory, the grand jury is a check against an irresponsible and malevolent prosecutor, as it can refuse to issue an indictment if the prosecutor's evidence seems insufficient. In practice, however, grand juries have no investigatory staff, no funds, and no independent counsel; usually they are merely "rubber stamps" for the prosecutors. About half the states no longer have grand juries. Felony charges in these states are initiated by a prosecutor's information.

Once a formal charge is issued against a person, especially for misdemeanors and less serious charges, a summons may issue to direct the defendant to appear in court for arraignment. For the more serious offenses, or if the defendant has failed to respond to a summons, an indictment warrant or an arrest warrant can be used to bring the defendant into court.

Arraignment: Counsel, Bail, and Pleas

Especially when he has been arrested, the defendant is entitled to an arraignment as soon as possible.

At the arraignment a judicial officer formally informs the defendant of the charge(s) and inquires into several critical questions, counsel, bail, and pleas.

Counsel. First and foremost is the matter of *legal counsel* for the accused. Our legal system operates as an *adversary* system. The theory is that, when two vigorous adversaries, one representing society and one representing the accused, do battle and leave no stone unturned, justice will emerge from the dust if there is an impartial umpire to supervise the struggle and make the factual judgments.

As prosecutors are representatives of society as a whole, in theory their primary objective ought to be justice. However, prosecutors are generally elected officials, and they usually are elected on a "law and order" platform. In addition, prosecutors are often dependent upon the local police for their investigatory work, and police usually have a professional (and at times, under threat of lawsuit, financial) stake in seeing that an arrest leads to a conviction. For these reasons, ambitious prosecutors are often single-minded in their pursuit of convictions.

To counterbalance the prosecutor, the defendant has his own attorney. Anyone charged with a crime is entitled to an attorney of his own choosing; however, attorneys' fees (generally $1,000 to $5,000 for a felony case) are often beyond the financial means of some criminal defendants. In almost all criminal cases, the defendant is entitled to have counsel provided free of charge if the court, at arraignment, determines that the defendant is without sufficient finances and income to retain counsel. In some places, there are full-time public defenders, who are paid salaries by the county or the state and who defend indigent defendants. In other places, indigents are defended by private attorneys paid by the court for each case they take.

The quality of these various assigned counsels varies enormously, and defendants are rarely given any choice in the selection. Though the Constitution states that an accused is entitled to the "effective assistance of counsel," the courts have repeatedly refused to reverse convictions on this basis unless counsel was so bad as to constitute "a sham and a mockery." With the institutionalization and progress of public defender systems, in some jurisdictions it is the defendant with moderate means, sufficient to retain inexperienced and inexpensive counsel of his own choosing, who may suffer the most. The choice of a lawyer should be made with great care and deliberation.

There is no doubt that the wealthy defendant usually has greater access to justice because he can hire talented, experienced counsel and has unimpeded access to the assistance of investigators, researchers, and technical experts. Theoretically, all persons are entitled to "equal protection under the law," and indigent defendants are entitled to equal access to justice. In practice, it is cumbersome and difficult for public defenders to approach the court and beg for funds for all but the most basic expenses.

Bail. Once the matter of counsel is determined, the second critical question at arraignment is that of bail. *Bail* is the security that a defendant gives to assure the court that he will not leave the jurisdiction and will be available for trial and sentencing. Bail can usually be cash, bank accounts, real property deeds, or a bail bond. The latter works like an insurance policy: A bonding company determines that the defendant is likely to be available for trial, takes a nonrefundable premium from the defendant, and posts the required bond with the court. If the defendant fails to show up at any stage of the legal proceedings against him, the full amount of the bond will be forfeited to the court. It is like paying $500 for an insurance policy on a $5,000 car. In case of an auto accident, the insurance company is required to pay the full book value on the car.

Though the U.S. Constitution forbids "excessive bail," this term has never been defined. In many jurisdictions, bail is set in all but capital crimes (those with the death penalty). A defendant can be released on his own recognizance, where the court recognizes the defendant's promise that he will appear at subsequent proceedings. Low bail or personal recognizance is the general rule for minor offenses, or for situations where the defendant is a long-time local resident, with steady employment, family, property, and an insignificant criminal record. The seriousness of the crime is supposed to be one factor in the equation.

Aside from the inconvenience and stigma of being held in jail for weeks and months before being convicted, the issue of bail can be crucial to the ultimate prospects of a criminal case. A defendant who is released on bail or personal recognizance often has better opportunities to assist in the preparation of a defense and also a better likelihood of demonstrating some personal rehabilitation as an alternative to a sentence of incarceration. The initial bail hearing at arraignment should, therefore, never be approached half-heartedly. Character references, family members, and thorough information should be presented to the court.

Pleas. The final question at arraignment is the entry of a *plea*, usually either guilty, not guilty, or nolo contendere (no contest). Most defendants should and do initially plead not guilty; in fact, this is automatic in some jurisdictions. A plea of nolo contendere subjects the defendant to the same punishment as a guilty plea, but a nolo plea does not technically admit guilt. It rather says the defendant does not contest the charges against him.

A plea of guilty or nolo contendere may be offered at any time before a verdict is rendered by a judge or jury after a trial. Before accepting a guilty plea, a judge must make inquiry to determine that the defendant is acting voluntarily and understands what he is doing.

Relevant questions a judge may ask before accepting a guilty plea include: Is the plea a result of any threats or promises? Does the defendant understand the right to trial, the right to confront witnesses, and the right to remain silent, all of which are being relinquished by pleading guilty? Has the defendant had satisfactory assistance of counsel? Has a plea bargain been made, and does the defendant understand its legal import? If this inquiry is not made, the defendant may later attempt to challenge the validity of the guilty plea, even after he receives a prison sentence.

Approximately seventy to eighty-five percent of defendants plead guilty, either at arraignment or at some subsequent time. Most often, the guilty plea is a result of *plea bargaining* between the prosecutor and the defense attorney. Under the unfairly maligned system of plea bargaining, the prosecutor recommends to the judge a reduction of the charge or a more lenient sentence in return for the defendant's waiver of his right to trial.

Both sides are usually well-served by this arrangement. As the number of criminal cases would overwhelm the system if all defendants exercised their rights to trial, the system is dependent upon plea bargaining. In addition, the prosecutor can spare the victim the trauma of a court appearance, and can guarantee a conviction (with almost no possibility of reversal on appeal). In offering and making sentencing recommendations, the prosecutor has enormous power and enormous opportunities for abuse. Especially where prosecution is initiated by information or by a rubber-stamp grand jury, prosecutors may "overcharge," bringing charges excessively harsh or excessive in number, thereby beginning the bargaining process at an artificially inflated negotiating strength.

From the defense point of view, most defendants face

incontrovertible evidence; a trial would be of minimal utility. What these defendants want primarily is a less severe punishment. By pleading guilty, the defendant gets a "lenient" recommendation by the prosecutor, may get a reduction in the charge, keeps the victim (and the gory details) out of the judge's sight, and shows some remorse and shame for what he has done—all of which serve to mitigate the potential punishment.

Ironically, though, the institution of plea bargaining serves the guilty much better than the innocent; the latter are put in the difficult dilemma of whether to stand trial and expect no leniency if convicted. Prosecutors often will offer the best deals in the weakest (from their point of view) cases, thereby heightening the dilemma. In essence, plea bargaining means that there is a price tag on exercising one's right to a trial.

In some jurisdictions the judge is involved in the plea bargain; but in many places, the judge is not a party to the bargain and there is no guarantee that the judge will accept it. However, most judges recognize the harshness of disregarding a plea bargain if a defendant, in reliance upon it, has given up his right to trial. Practically speaking, if a judge acquires a reputation for occasionally disregarding recommendations for leniency, future defendants will be unlikely to plead guilty before that judge.

As long as the record reflects that a guilty plea was voluntary, intelligent, and made with the advice of counsel, there are usually no grounds for appeal if the defendant receives an undesired sentence.

Pre-Trial Proceedings

A Break for the Defendant. Occasionally, charges are dropped by the prosecution for one reason or another. If a critical witness cannot be located, the prosecution may have no choice in the matter. However, a victim or a witness is not a party in a criminal case. If a witness is a friend or relative of the defendant, or for some other reason is reluctant to press the charges and testify, the prosecutor has the power to subpoena the witness and ask for a bench warrant for that witness' arrest if he does not appear voluntarily.

Once the witness is in court, the prosecutor can call him to the witness stand and ask the judge to force the witness to testify under threat of being held in contempt of court. For practical reasons, prosecutors usually avoid relying upon reluctant witnesses.

There are various mechanisms for dropping charges. Some of them can be done behind the scenes by the unilateral action of the prosecutor. Others are more public, and therefore less subject to both corruption and suspicion, such as a dismissal by a judge upon the recommendation of the prosecutor.

In some jurisdictions, especially for minor offenses and younger defendants, a defendant with no prior criminal record may have an opportunity to have a charge dismissed—essentially by an act of mercy—possibly after a waiting or continued period of time to see if he stays out of further trouble. Alternatively, this approach may be taken in conjunction with some further court order, such as restitution to the victim, community service work, or the imposition of some restrictions on the defendant's life-style.

Preliminary Hearing. Many defendants choose not to plead guilty at the outset, and the arraignment is often the beginning of a process that may take several years if there is a trial and subsequent appeal. Especially if the defendant is to be held in custody on bail, courts of most jurisdictions require that there be a *screening function*—an independent finding of probable cause to believe the defendant is guilty of the crime charged—before subjecting him to the agony of this long process.

If the defendant has been indicted by a grand jury, that

body has theoretically found probable cause against the defendant, thereby justifying the further proceedings. The deficiencies of grand juries have already been discussed. Courts have generally refused to inquire into the sufficiency or nature (such as hearsay) of the evidence on which the grand jury based the indictment.

When the prosecution has been initiated by a complaint or an information, most states provide for a "preliminary examination" or "probable cause hearing" before a judicial officer who determines whether there is probable cause. Even states with grand juries often initiate many prosecutions with complaints or informations; most of these states also provide preliminary examinations prior to the grand jury proceedings.

Generally speaking, a finding of "no probable cause," though it terminates the particular case and discharges the defendant, is not a legal bar to a subsequent complaint, information, or indictment. In any event, not many preliminary examinations result in a finding of no probable cause. Many of the judicial officers who preside at such hearings have insufficient legal training and independence to short-circuit the prosecution at that stage. Experienced defense lawyers in many jurisdictions rarely, if ever, present any defense evidence at a preliminary examination.

Though its screening function is often more illusory than real, the preliminary examination is often critical as a tool of *discovery* for the defense. As the investigation has been in the hands of the prosecution, the preliminary examination is the first opportunity for defense counsel to see, hear, and cross-examine at least some of the prosecution witnesses. Counsel can thereby evaluate the case in detail; in addition, if the testimony of the witnesses is inconsistent with their testimony later at trial, the inconsistencies can often be pointed out at the trial to cast doubt on the witnesses' credibility.

Because of these opportunities for defense counsel, the preliminary examination provides a significant tactical ad-

vantage over a grand jury, where testimony is often per-
functory and defense counsel does not participate. Though
the defendant is entitled to counsel at a preliminary examination, many inexperienced defense attorneys fail to take
advantage of the discovery potential of these hearings.

Other Pre-Trial Discovery. Theoretically, the defense is
entitled to investigate the case in the same manner as the
prosecution, except for the subpoena power of grand juries.
However, prosecution witnesses often feel that they have
some sort of a stake in the conviction of the defendant; and
they are often reluctant to talk to defense investigators. Besides, the defense is usually investigating weeks or months
after the crime; and the defense may have, at best, extremely
limited investigatory resources, certainly nothing similar to a
police force. For these reasons, it is often quite difficult to
prepare a defense without a thorough preliminary examination.

Some prosecutors will voluntarily and informally turn
over other discovery materials, such as names and addresses
of witnesses, prior written statements of prosecution witnesses, prior statements of the defendant, physical evidence,
any details of any lineup or other identification process.

If the desired information is not turned over informally,
the defense must file a motion requesting that the court
order that the prosecution turn it over. Though the defendant is entitled to the effective assistance of counsel, and the
Supreme Court has recognized that counsel must have an
opportunity to acquaint himself with the facts of the case,
jurisdictions vary immensely in the amount and nature of
discovery that must be provided by the prosecution. Until
recently, criminal practice was treated as a game where sur-
prise was a legitimate weapon. However, there has been a
recent trend to mandate greater discovery of basic items such
as grand jury testimony.

If the prosecutor has evidence favorable to the accused,

he is legally obligated to turn it over to defense counsel. This rule, however, leaves much room for judgmental questions; and it is rarely followed with excessive diligence.

There has also been a recent movement, especially in places where discovery is being opened up for the defense, to mandate certain discovery for the prosecution from the defense, such as the names of defense expert or alibi witnesses.

Other Pre-Trial Tactics and Motions. Many other legal issues are often raised before a judge prior to the commencement of a trial. Especially if the case is highly publicized, the defense may request a change of *venue*, a change in the location of the trial, usually to another county. If the defense can show that some adverse publicity has emanated from the police or prosecutor, counsel may ask the court to dismiss the charges. If neither of these solutions is granted, the jury may be locked up or *sequestered* during the trial and sheltered from any publicity about the case.

There are numerous other grounds on which a case may be dismissed or "quashed" upon the defendant's motion. Among them are: the inadequacy of the jurors or grand jurors because of underrepresentation of some population group; the unconstitutionality, because it is too vague or because it invades constitutionally protected behavior, of the statute under which the defendant is charged; technical inadequacies in the indictment, such as its failure adequately to inform the defendant of what he is charged with; and "former jeopardy" or "double jeopardy," meaning that the defendant has previously been prosecuted for the identical offense. (Double jeopardy does not, however, apply to prosecution by both state and federal authorities for the same offense.)

A pre-trial issue raised quite frequently is the right of the defendant, under the U.S. Constitution and most state constitutions, to a "speedy trial." A defendant who wants to push for a speedy trial can file a motion requesting one. The remedy for denial of a speedy trial is usually dismissal of the charges. Because many delays are caused or welcomed by defendants and their counsel, sometimes for legitimate needs such as preparation and sometimes just to stall, courts have evolved extremely flexible rules in this area. The foremost factors considered are the length of the delay, the reason for the delay, the defendant's efforts (or lack thereof) to obtain a speedy trial, and the prejudice to the defendant because of the delay. Special priority is given to defendants in custody awaiting trial, since the prejudice to them is so obvious.

Motions to Exclude Evidence

In 1961 the U.S. Supreme Court, in a controversial decision (*Mapp v. Ohio*), ruled that any material obtained by unlawful acts of law enforcement officials is excluded, or inadmissible as evidence, in the subsequent criminal trial. The court reasoned that other sanctions, such as civil suits against police, are "worthless and futile" to deter official illegality; and they stated that "nothing can destroy a government more quickly than its failure to observe its own laws."

To take advantage of this rule, the defendant, if his counsel is aware of the unlawfully gathered evidence, files a pre-trial Motion to Suppress (or Exclude) the evidence. This motion is generally heard by a judge before the trial commences. Both sides present witnesses, and the judge decides whether the evidence is admissible. In three areas, those of search and seizure of evidence, Fifth Amendment rights, and identification procedures, the judge's decision can be critical to the outcome of the trial that will follow. In many cases, if the evidence is excluded, the prosecution has no choice but to request dismissal of the charges.

Search and Seizure. Physical evidence, such as contraband (at times even the contraband that is the basis of the charges) or items taken as evidence of guilt, may be excluded from evidence if the defense can show that they were taken in violation of the Fourth Amendment to the U.S. Constitution, which forbids "unreasonable searches and seizures." Under the same principle, if items are seized as a result of an illegal arrest, the items are excluded from the trial.

The law in this area is constantly in a state of flux, but there are certain general justifications for a search and seizure. If an item is in the "plain view" of a police officer who is not committing an invasion of anyone's privacy, then there is technically no search and the item can be seized.

A valid search warrant is the legally preferred justification for a search. Like an arrest warrant, a search warrant is issued by a judicial officer who hears facts constituting probable cause that a person has contraband or items that are evidence of illegal behavior. Most applications for search warrants are routinely approved. Unlike an arrest warrant, a search warrant must be accompanied by an affidavit signed by the person, usually a police officer, who possesses and presents the alleged probable cause to the judicial official.

A defendant who later challenges the sufficiency of the search often challenges that affidavit. The most common challenges are to the sufficiency of the facts in the affidavit constituting probable cause or to the truthfulness of the facts therein.

The Fourth Amendment also states that warrants must particularly describe the place to be searched and the persons or things to be seized. If the warrant appears to authorize a general, exploratory search, then the warrant is illegal. Similarly, if the items are seized in an area not authorized by the warrant, such as in a different apartment of the same building, then the warrant does not serve to justify the seizure. In addition, a search warrant cannot be executed after a reasonable amount of time has elapsed. Under all these circumstances, the items seized would be excluded from the trial unless there exists another justification for their seizure.

Other than a warrant, there are numerous justifications for searches and seizures. If the officers are making a lawful arrest, they are entitled to search the arrestee and the area in his immediate control. Also, anybody with authority over an area can consent to a search of that area, as long as the consent is voluntary and intelligent. Consent is valid though the person giving it is unaware of his right to say no or is subtly intimidated by the officiality of the officer who requests permission to search. If the officer actually threatens or misleads the person, the consent is not voluntary and it will not justify the search and seizure.

Police are also authorized to search someone or someplace if, first, they have probable cause to believe that items connected with criminal activity will be found in the place to be searched and if, second, there exists "exigent circumstances" making it impossible to take the time to get a search warrant. Automobile and airplane searches are frequently justified on this basis.

Again, probable cause can be based upon hearsay information, even from an unnamed informant, so long as the informant's reliability is apparent, and especially if the officers' own observations corroborate the information they receive.

Finally, though the police lack probable cause to search somebody, they generally are entitled to question a person whom they merely suspect of illegality (though the person generally need not answer). If, upon questioning the person, the police acquire some reason to suspect that the person may be armed and dangerous, then the police have authority to *frisk* the person, to pat down the outer clothing. If the frisk indicates an object which may be a weapon, the officer is entitled to intrude beneath the surface of the clothing to determine what the object is. The criteria for each step must be met if the search is challenged later in a motion to exclude the evidence.

If a search is deemed valid, then any items seized in the

course of that search will be admissible into evidence, whether or not they are the items originally sought by the police and whether or not the originally sought items are found at all.

If, on the other hand, the search is deemed illegal, then any evidence, tangible or intangible, obtained as a result of the illegal search will be excluded from the trial as "fruit of the poisonous tree." The same rule applies to evidence obtained as a result of illegally obtained confessions.

The Fifth Amendment. Confessions, oral or written, of a criminal defendant may not be used in evidence unless there was a valid *waiver* of the defendant's Fifth Amendment right against self-incrimination before the statement was made. The first hurdle for a waiver is that it be voluntary and not coerced. If the defendant can show, usually contrary to the testimony of the police, that he was subjected to force, threats, excessively harsh confinement, and the like, then any confession that resulted may be excluded from evidence, because our legal system conclusively presumes that such a confession is unreliable.

The next hurdle is that the defendant must, to validly waive the Fifth Amendment rights, understand those rights. Under the 1966 Supreme Court decision in *Miranda v. Arizona*, if the police question a defendant who is in custody, then the defendant's responses are not admissible in evidence unless, to begin with, the police first inform him (1) that he has the right to remain silent, (2) that anything he says can be used against him in court, (3) that he has the right to consult an attorney and to have an attorney with him during the interrogation, and (4) that if he is indigent an attorney will be appointed to represent him. If the defendant is not in custody, or if the confession is blurted out without any police questioning, then the *Miranda* rule is of no avail to the defendant.

If, on the other hand, the rule applies, then the prosecution must show that the defendant demonstrated an understanding of these rights and of his free will, chose to disregard them. Especially if the defendant is young, retarded, or under the influence of drugs or alcohol, the prosecution may have a hard time showing that a confession was voluntary and that the constitutional rights were intelligently waived.

The Fifth Amendment privilege also protects a person from giving self-incriminatory testimony in a legal proceeding such as a grand jury hearing or a trial. A person need not answer any questions that will tend to furnish a link in the chain of evidence needed to convict him of a crime. If a judge finds that a person is clearly mistaken in asserting the privilege, then the person can be held in contempt unless he answers the question.

If the person has a valid Fifth Amendment claim, he can still be compelled to testify if he is granted *immunity from prosecution*. In some jurisdictions this is immunity only from having the prosecution use the person's testimony in a subsequent trial; in others, the immunity is much broader and more valuable, immunizing the person from prosecution for any offense to which the question is related.

It should be noted that the Fifth Amendment privilege does not cover "nontestimonial" evidence extracted from the defendant, such as blood tests, fingerprints, handwriting samples, or forcing the defendant to stand in a lineup. A person legally in custody may be forced to undergo these procedures.

Identification Procedures. The Supreme Court has recognized that mistaken identification causes more injustices than almost any other problem in the criminal field. The procedures by which a defendant is identified are, therefore, often the subject of constitutional scrutiny. If a person has been formally charged with a crime, then any identification procedure must take place with the knowledge and, if the accused wishes, the presence of defense counsel.

If the procedure takes place, as most do, before the formal charges are lodged, the courts will scrutinize the procedure to determine whether it was "unnecessarily suggestive," creating an unfair likelihood that the defendant was chosen. For example, a black suspect in an all-white lineup would obviously be and historically has intentionally been suggestive.

Short of this, however, the standards are uncertain and unstable. A lineup is certainly not required, and photographic identification is usually adequate as long as it is conducted fairly. Generally, a more suggestive procedure, such as a one-person "showup," is acceptable if it is conducted promptly after the alleged crime.

Occasionally, the defendant may convince a judge (again, in a hearing on a pre-trial motion to exclude the evidence) that the out-of-court identification was unfair. In such a case, it will be excluded, that is, the jury will not hear of it. However, an in-court identification by the witnesses is nevertheless often permitted, if the prosecution can show that it is not the "fruit of the poisonous tree" but is made independently of, as opposed to being caused by, the unlawful out-of-court procedure.

TRIAL

Judge or Jury

If the charges have not been dropped for some reason, anyone who continues to plead not guilty must eventually have a trial to seek exoneration. In some jurisdictions one is entitled to a trial by jury for all offenses, even minor charges such as traffic violations where only a fine may be imposed. In other places, minor offenses must be tried by a judge. The Supreme Court has ruled that, under the U.S. Constitution, a person is entitled to a jury trial only if he is in jeopardy of going to jail for more than six months.

In most instances, one is entitled to waive one's right to a jury trial and have a trial with a judge as the fact-finder. A trial by a judge is often much quicker and more informal than a jury trial because the judge is theoretically less susceptible to improper influences and fewer procedural steps are required. In many jurisdictions, a defendant is more likely to trust a jury for an independent decision on a disputed factual matter. Judges are usually politically sensitive, and criminal defendants are less popular than victims and police officers. However, with some judges or with a particularly complex, technical, gruesome, or sensitive case it may be advisable to waive one's right to a jury.

The jury system has a somewhat exaggerated mystique as our principal defense against oppressive government. Most jury trials are decided by juries of twelve people, but occasionally fewer than twelve are used, especially for lesser offenses. The Supreme Court has approved of juries as small as six people. The jury is chosen randomly from a larger pool called the *venire*, which consists of citizens from the county in which the court and trial are located. They are often chosen randomly from a list such as the voter registration list. In some places, especially rural areas, they are chosen more informally, often with more "discretion" in the hands of some local official.

Under the Sixth Amendment to the U.S. Constitution, one is entitled to "an impartial jury"; some state constitutions refer to a jury of one's "peers." The Supreme Court has held that a jury, to be impartial, must be selected "from a cross-section of the community." However, only in cases where important population groups, such as black people or women, were intentionally excluded from the venire have the state courts ruled that the venire was unfair.

Thus, if a group is excluded because of supposedly rational selection criteria—such as character, literacy, or property requirements—the venire is considered satisfactory. In fact, jury venires in many jurisdictions are, for an accumulation of ostensibly rational criteria, extremely unrepresentative of the population at large. In many places, professional people—teachers, doctors, lawyers—are routinely excused. Especially if voter lists are used, young people, transients (such as college students), and poor people are often not included. Though many defendants are from poor and/or minority backgrounds, very few jurors are. Thus it is more likely than not that the defendant will not be judged by a jury of his peers.

Once the twelve (or fewer) jurors are chosen from the venire, there is a process called *voire dire* to question the prospective jurors and determine whether any of them are biased. In some jurisdictions this process is conducted by the judge; but in some places it is done, especially in capital cases, by counsel under the guidance of the judge.

If the judge agrees that a juror is biased, the juror is excused "for cause." Each side also has a certain number of *peremptory challenges* that it can use to excuse jurors without giving any reason. Jury selection has, in recent years, become increasingly susceptible to the assistance of sociological and psychological experts. Only the defendant with financial resources can avail himself of such assistance.

Confronting the Witness

After the jury is selected, the prosecutor (and possibly the defense counsel, as well) offers an opening statement summarizing the evidence. Next the prosecutor calls his witnesses. The Constitution states that the trial shall be "public"; however, in particularly distasteful or indecent cases the court may, especially if the defendant assents, exclude the general public from the trial.

Under the Sixth Amendment to the U.S. Constitution, a defendant is guaranteed the right to confront, which means to cross-examine, the witness against him. Cross-examination—though its value may be exaggerated in the popular mythology derived from fictional characters such as

Perry Mason—is at once the most fundamental and the most difficult skill of trial lawyers. Because the Supreme Court has recognized the important protective value of cross-examination, hearsay (evidence of things said off the witness stand) is almost never admitted in a criminal case.

Rules of Evidence

There are many other rules of evidence, besides the hearsay rule, that govern the trial. In an attempt to avoid the presentation of improper, prejudicial evidence, the witnesses are not permitted to narrate the facts in their own words. Instead, they must answer individual questions, so that the opposing counsel can have an opportunity to object to questions he believes to be unfair. It then becomes the judge's responsibility to decide whether the question is proper and the witness may answer.

At times, a witness makes unfair and prejudicial statements before anyone can prevent it; the judge should then instruct the jury to disregard the statement. Often this procedure actually heightens the prejudicial effect. If the judge feels that the prejudice was especially serious, a *mistrial* can be declared, and the trial must start over again with a different jury.

The Prosecution's Burden of Proof

Under a traditional rule made binding upon all jurisdictions by the Supreme Court, the prosecution has the burden of proving guilt. Another way of saying this is that the defendant is "innocent until proven guilty." This means that the prosecution must convince the fact-finder (jury or judge) that the defendant was responsible for each and every element, both the acts and mental elements, necessary to be considered guilty of the charge.

Usually the prosecution's burden is to prove guilt "beyond a reasonable doubt" or beyond a moral certainty. If the jurors (or judge) have a doubt to which they can attach a reason, then they are obligated to render a not guilty verdict. Even if the defense raises an affirmative defense, such as self-defense or insanity, it is the prosecution's burden to prove the absence of these defenses.

In practical reality, however, both a judge and a jury at least subconsciously assume that the defendant is before them for *some* reason. Because defendants are often uneducated, from minority heritages, and poor, they are often faced with fear and prejudice, which leads to certain other conclusions that at least partially obviate the principle that the defendant is innocent without proof of guilt. It is far more accurate to say that the defendant must prove his innocence, overcoming prejudicial assumptions of his possible guilt.

The defendant, in theory at least, need not take the witness stand and need not put on any evidence to try to prove his innocence. Because of the Fifth Amendment, the prosecutor cannot attempt to call the defendant as a witness, nor can the prosecutor comment upon the defendant's failure to take the witness stand in his own behalf. Usually the jury is instructed, at the close of the case, not to draw any adverse inference from the defendant's silence.

However, the decision whether the defendant should take the witness stand is not so simple. Regardless of the theoretical and legal rules, jurors in many cases will undoubtedly be wondering why the defendant has remained silent if he is truly innocent. In fact, there are numerous reasons why an innocent defendant may, on the advice of counsel, decline to take the witness stand.

Many defendants are not articulate and well-educated: to jurors of different backgrounds, such a defendant may sound foreign and untrustworthy. In most jurisdictions a defendant's criminal record will be disclosed to the jury if and only if the defendant testifies at the trial. Obviously this can have an enormous impact on the jury. This rule is justified on the basis that prior crimes indicate a propensity to the untruthful. The harshness of this rule is apparent; in some places the rule is watered down, such as to allow only prior crimes of deception and trickery to be cited.

As stated, the prosecution has the burden of proof. Thus, if the judge determines that on one or more essential elements of the alleged crime (even if all the prosecution evidence is believed) there is absolutely no evidence of guilt, the judge in theory may order or "direct" a verdict of not guilty.

If a directed verdict is not granted, the defense then chooses whether or not to exercise its constitutional right to call defense witnesses.

The Jury Verdict
After all the evidence has been presented, both sides have an opportunity to sum up their views of the evidence in closing arguments. In most places, the defense goes first and the prosecution gets the last word.

Prior to deliberating on their verdict, the jury receives the judge's instructions on the rules of law they are to apply in reaching a verdict. Among these will be the essential elements of the crimes, the definition of reasonable doubt, and an explanation of any defenses that have been raised. Either party can request that certain instructions be given; and the parties may object to portions of the instructions, often requesting that something be added.

In most jurisdictions, a jury verdict—whether guilty or not guilty—must be unanimous. The Supreme Court has, however, approved of non-unanimous verdicts (9-3 and 10-2) established by law in a few places. If the jurors cannot agree on a verdict, a mistrial is declared and the defendant must await another jury trial, unless the prosecution decides to drop the charges.

Sentencing
If the defendant is found guilty, whether by guilty plea or by verdict of judge or jury, then the judge must impose a sentence limited only by the minimum and maximum sentences

prescribed by the law governing the offense in question.

At many steps of the criminal process there are elements of discretion and chance. Will the police officer make an arrest? Will the case be assigned to a hard-nosed prosecutor? Will the defense lawyer be skillful? Will he know the prosecutor or the judge? But nowhere in the process is there a greater roulette wheel than in the judge's sentencing. It is widely agreed that different judges might give widely disparate sentences in identical cases.

Occasionally the legislature removes some of the judge's sentencing discretion, generally by imposing a mandatory sentence to prison. Although such laws remove some of the sentencing disparities, they are often harsh, as they also preclude the consideration of exceptional and mitigating circumstances.

The range of possible sentences is usually quite wide, beginning with a monetary fine (paid to the court) or, especially where the victim has suffered financial loss, restitution (paid to the victim). Payment of fines and restitution may be combined with other kinds of sentences, such as probation.

When a person is put on *probation* for a period of time he remains under the court's power or jurisdiction. Generally speaking he must not only stay out of further criminal difficulties, but also report regularly to a probation officer employed by the court. In addition, the judge can impose specific conditions of probation, such as steady employment or residence in a halfway house for drug addicts. If a probationer wants to move to another county or another state, he must get permission from the probation officer. Arrangements are usually made for supervision to continue in the new county or state.

If any of the conditions of probation is violated while the probation is still in effect, the subject can be summonsed back (or brought in by an arrest) to the sentencing court for a hearing on the alleged violation. If, after the hearing, a judge finds that the probation has been violated, the defendant is entitled to a hearing, after which he can be resentenced to anything within the limits of the original law under which the defendant was convicted.

Sometimes a judge will impose, along with the supervision of probation, a suspended sentence to prison. Then if the probation is violated, the specific suspended sentence is put into effect. In practice, there is little difference between a suspended sentence and "straight probation," except for the certainty of the former.

Alternatively, the defendant can be incarcerated in a county jail or a state prison. The latter must be used for the most serious felonies. State prisons, therefore, contain the most hardened and vicious criminals of each state; and the security procedures at state prisons are usually more stringent than those of county jails.

In many jurisdictions, at least in theory, efforts are made to facilitate the rehabilitation of prisoners. Psychological counselling, educational programs, and job training are sometimes offered. But our society has never committed any significant resources over a significant time period to these efforts. On the whole, our prison system serves mostly to keep prisoners locked up. If anything, our prisons increase criminal tendencies by putting people in brutalizing environments with other hardened criminals. Prison sentences in the U.S. are, contrary to popular mythology, long compared with those of other nations.

In most places, a prisoner is entitled to be released on parole after a portion of his sentence has expired, especially if the prison authorities are pleased with his behavior in prison. The decision is usually in the hands of a state parole board, a body generally appointed by the governor.

Parole functions much like probation: A parole officer supervises the parolee, and his liberty is conditioned upon such factors as good behavior. If the terms of parole are violated, the parolee is entitled to a hearing, after which he can be returned to the prison to finish the original sentence.

If the violation is not considered serious enough, the parolee can be given a chance to remain out on parole until the maximum sentence is completed and he is discharged from any further obligation for his crime.

Finally, capital punishment exists in some states for some crimes, particularly murder. The Supreme Court has recently ruled that the death penalty is not inherently "cruel and unusual punishment," which is otherwise prohibited by the Eighth Amendment of the U.S. Constitution. Though there is no solid evidence that the death penalty serves as a greater deterrent to crime than life imprisonment, the Court has ruled that states are entitled to employ the death penalty as long as the criteria for its imposition are set out by law rather than being open-ended and discretionary.

Sentencing is a much-neglected aspect of the criminal process. Experienced defense counsel can have an oft-neglected effect upon the sentencing by presenting to the judge family members, employers, teachers, character references, or programs that will serve as alternatives to incarceration.

Appeal

Once a judge or jury has entered a guilty verdict, the defendant can usually appeal only legal, as opposed to factual, questions that were disputed before and during the trial. If there are substantial issues under federal statutes or the federal Constitution, the defendant may be able to appeal a state conviction to the federal appellate courts, including the Supreme Court. The defendant is entitled to the assistance of counsel to help him in the appeal.

Appellate courts generally are reluctant to overrule the decisions of the judge who presided at the trial. Occasionally, if the defendant appears to have a substantial appellate issue, a stay of sentence is ordered to await the decision on the appeal.

Finally, a defendant serving a sentence can apply to the

governor to have the sentence *commuted*, which means that the sentence is completely ended and the defendant is discharged without parole supervision. Alternatively, the governor or the President has the discretionary power to grant a *pardon*, which not only discharges the defendant but also wipes the defendant's record clean.

CONCLUSION

It should be apparent that the criminal process is a highly complex and increasingly specialized legal field. The safeguards erected to protect the innocent are among the most elaborate in the world, because our system presumes that it is better that an occasional guilty person go free than that many innocent people get convicted.

However, much of the public is under the misconception that lawbreakers by the score go free because of technicalities and misguided bleeding-hearts. Anyone with everyday experience in the field of criminal law knows that such is not the case, primarily because more than seventy percent of all defendants plead guilty. In addition, most judges bend over backwards to avoid setting defendants free on technicalities; and many appellate courts, though they find legal errors in a trial, rule (basically on their own speculation) that the errors were "harmless" in the jury's deliberations.

As for the segment of public opinion demanding more and longer prison sentences, again the reality is at odds with the myth, for ultimately prison sentences are counterproductive when imposed without being thoroughly justified. Even the hardest-nosed judges and prosecutors recognize the fact that many criminals who pass through the revolving court doors are not totally responsible for their own fates; much of crime is a product of social and economic deprivation. Many criminals are more pathetic than dangerous.

Our ultimate mistake is to rely upon the criminal justice

system to attempt to cure crime. It cannot cure crime any more than it can create crime. Crime is a function of our society as a whole. Our criminal justice system should be relied upon only to provide justice. And that task is none too small.

10

Choosing a Lawyer

In any legal proceeding, the lawyer you select will have a significant effect, not only on the outcome of your case but also upon your personal feelings and your purse as well. It is not true that if you've seen one lawyer you've seen them all; nor is it true that all lawyers are dishonest, charge exorbitant fees, or are faultless saints.

In fact, lawyers are diverse human beings and provide services of varying quality in many different fields. Some lawyers are totally inappropriate to handle certain types of problems. Therefore, which lawyer you go to will depend in part upon the kind of situation with which you need help.

THE GENERAL PRACTITIONER OR THE SPECIALIST

The majority of lawyers today are general practitioners. They are equipped to handle a broad variety of legal work, whether it is a will, a criminal case, a lawsuit, or a small business. For the average person with a need for a lawyer, the general practitioner attorney will be sufficient.

To cite an example, most divorces are settled by negotiation and compromise; and a contested court battle between husband and wife is seldom necessary. Many times there is no dispute whatsoever, and the husband and wife merely want a severance of their legal ties. There may be no children involved, no alimony requested, and no property to divide. In such cases, going to a divorce specialist from a fancy downtown firm may be unnecessary and an excessive expense. The general practitioner should be able to accomplish the same result for such clients as the specialist, but at a much lower fee and perhaps with a more personable approach.

Most general practitioners are quite candid in admitting to their clients areas in which their expertise may be deficient. In such instances, they usually will refer these cases out to a specialist in whom they have confidence, much as a general doctor might refer his patient who has a bad heart to a heart specialist. All general lawyers are trained to spot a problem accurately, and they usually know when it is too complicated for them to handle.

Some lawyers freely admit that they do not do, for example, corporate work, or tax work, or estate work. Other lawyers do nothing but one specific type of work. The sensible thing to do is to ask your lawyer at the outset if he handles your particular type of case.

Some problems are particularly intricate. Their complications and possible consequences make a specialist necessary. Until very recently, lawyers were not (with the exceptions of admiralty and patent lawyers) allowed to hold themselves out to the public as specialists. Instead, they more or less had to develop reputations through word-of-mouth, other lawyers, and publicity. This was a most unreliable and spotty system; and people in genuine need of a specialist had little help in finding a competent attorney.

Within the last year, both the listing of specialists and lawyer advertising have become the hottest topics of controversy within the local, state, and national bar associations. Some states, most recently the state of Maine, have liberally approved of both of these innovations. Most other states are debating the specialist proposition, although the general populace and even the courts seem to be of the opinion that silence contributes to a monopoly, public ignorance, and a lack of public concern. The U.S. Supreme Court recently declared that outright state bans on lawyer advertising are prohibited. Exactly what is permissable in the light of that decision is what is the subject of the greatest dissention in each of the fifty state bar associations who regulate the conduct of attorneys in their respective states.

ADVERTISING AND FEES

The trend appears to be leading to some form of limited advertising, at first making available listings of specialists in the telephone books and other directories. This will make it much easier for people to find the lawyer they want and the lawyer they need.

Lawyers in many states are now advertising their fees in advance. Some attorneys argue that cases have too many individual considerations that may take additional time, research, and study, and that projected fees are therefore unreliable. A will can be one page or fifty pages, depending upon the needs and wishes of the testator. Of what use is it to any client to know that a certain lawyer's fees for wills *begin* at $75? Until the lawyer hears of the particular circumstances of each client, it is argued that he can really have no accurate way to predict the costs of his labor; and advertising prior to consultation would too often be misleading and hence of little value in gauging price.

Contrary to the arguments propounded by the bar associations, the Supreme Court decided that advertising would not undermine professionalism, would aid new attorneys entering the market, would reduce the cost of legal services, and was the constitutional right of every attorney. The individual state bar associations, dominated by established lawyers, are generally reacting to the Court's decision by implementing guidelines greatly limiting the permissible methods of advertising. Future Court decisions are inevitable before the matter is more finally determined.

It should be noted that prior to discussing anything with a lawyer you are entitled to ascertain what his hourly rate would be for an initial consultation. Some lawyers charge little or nothing for a visit to discuss the feasability of a new case. Others will charge upwards of a hundred dollars. It is wise to ask before the consultation begins.

Once the attorney has evaluated your case in the initial visit, it is then appropriate to ask for a range or approximation of what he would project your legal fees to be. Some lawyers may even put this estimate in writing, with the understanding that it is only an estimate. For example, if the case is settled without his having to try the matter in court, the fee might be considerably less than his original estimate. Or a case may consume much more time than could have been initially projected, and he will have to charge a higher fee. Most lawyers, however, will stay within the range indicated in the initial conference. They have reputations in the community to keep up and are usually aware of the commitments they have made to their clients.

It is the client who never asks about his fee until the conclusion of the case who is shocked and dismayed over his bill. Like the citizen who chooses not to vote, he really has little claim for unfair treatment as a result of his silence. Everyone visiting a lawyer (or a doctor, a contractor, or any other service person) should be clear on price before he agrees to be served by that person.

The coming of advertising cannot help but keep the

public educated and informed, and it should ultimately result in a public less bitter about its treatment by the legal community. Lawyers with established clientele and with established firms tend to be its chief opponents for obvious reasons.

Members of the larger law firms tend to dominate most bar associations. The typical small practitioner has little time to devote to outside activities like the bar, while the larger firms often make it a policy to assign one or more of their members to active bar association functions. Thus, for example, these large firms with already established clientele often have a vested commercial interest in opposing full legal advertising, an innovation that would do them little good. This may in part account for the organized bars' nearly uniform opposition to it.

LARGE FIRM OR SOLE PRACTITIONER

Black, Slack, Flack, and Quack may be one of the highly reputed law firms on Broad Street, Wall Street, or State Street. They may employ forty full-time lawyers, have the top two floors of the city's tallest insurance company building, and serve coffee and donuts in their plush, panoramic waiting room. They may make you feel like you are *someone*; and for many people, this movie-set illusion is important. It represents status, security, and tradition.

If you are one of those people, you should remember that the sofa, the view, and the bank of secretaries are not free; as a client of such a firm, you are paying your proportionate share of these expensive perquisites. It does not necessarily mean that the lawyers affiliated with that office are any more competent than the two lawyers on the other side of town practicing in an older office building with cracked leather chairs.

In reality, those other lawyers may be more approachable, personable, and downright too busy or unaffected to be bothered with decor and donuts. Much of running a law office can be a show, designed to impress the client with visible but irrelevant signs of success. Symbols can be very expensive, and usually they are meaningless.

On the other hand, large law firms have tremendous resources available to them. Having a large number of lawyers in the same office allows degrees of specialization within the firm, a luxury unavailable to the sole practitioner. Also, in a case that is in the process of trial, the larger firms often have a tactical advantage. They can file a huge number of motions, pleadings, depositions, and the like, and in the process wear down a small law office with their superior capital, manpower, and time. Because large firms often attract wealthier clients for whom money is no object, they will by design consume large amounts of court time, which the smaller firms and poorer clients cannot possibly match.

However, this is a double-edged sword. Sole practitioners and small firms tend to be more amenable to reasonably settling a case if it is possible to do so. Their approach is often more humane and is directed toward limiting the damages inherent in a protracted dispute. Larger firms, on the other hand, may be less readily disposed, because of their resources and available expenses, to end a dispute in a compromise but may instead prefer to go all out in a costly court battle. Their clients may possibly even be unaware that the case was susceptible at some point to a settlement.

This is not a blanket condemnation of large law firms. Many are honest and are competitively priced with smaller firms. But because of their size and expense of operation, they may tend to be more costly, more disposed to litigation, and potentially more effective in certain types of actions. For example, they may have their own trust department; and if you wish to draw a complex trust, a large firm may be most appropriate.

The sole general practitioner is educated to know a little

about everything. The sole specialist practitioner is in business only for a certain type of law. In either case, the sole practitioner is generally a person who has made it on his own through hard work, determination, and the slow construction of a viable law practice. He could not be where he is without being somewhat successful at representing his clients over the years.

Many sole practitioners share office space with a few other attorneys. Each attorney has his own clients, but the lawyers sharing the space, rent, and library facilities often consult with each other on cases within their respective realms of experience. For example, one of them might have expertise in home conveyancing while another might have had a great deal of work involving automobile torts. They will pool their knowledge where appropriate, which operates to the distinct benefit of their clients. This type of office combines the best of both worlds: It provides the lower fees and more personable approach often associated with a sole practitioner or small office with the special expertise and facilities of a larger firm.

It can be a tremendous comfort to develop a long-term relationship with a sole practitioner, particularly one in the general practice of law. He will serve you when you buy a house, when you adopt a child, when death strikes your family, and when you need advice to get out of a jam. He becomes a part of your family in a way in which Black, Slack, Flack, and Quack never really can.

CITY LAWYER OR LOCAL LAWYER

Many people erroneously feel that they must go to the largest city in their state and then to its most prestigious legal district in order to receive top-notch legal services. City lawyers in truth are no more or less competent than lawyers in the suburbs or lawyers in the country.

Most of what has previously been discussed relative to large versus small firms is applicable to city versus local lawyers. Those lawyers who practice in urban centers must pay higher rent and also higher salaries to their legal and clerical help. These added costs must be passed on to the clients. There is also a greater pressure to maintain an impressive office in the city, a kind of "keep up with Jones & Jones" mentality. This, too, means higher fees.

Lawyers outside the city offer additional convenience. They are usually more immediately accessible. Parking is often much less of a problem outside the city. The location alone can save you precious hours for your own day.

More importantly, as a member of a small, local community, the lawyer is more aware of maintaining a reputation of honesty and integrity. He is more likely to be damaged economically by negative words about the way he handles cases than a city lawyer who is not intimately involved with his location. The local lawyer often lives in the same community in which he works, thereby further increasing his stake in retaining good will in the community.

On the other hand, most city lawyers are located where they are because it is central to the majority of their clients and is also close to the courts at which they predominantly practice. There are many city lawyers who are competitively priced with the surburban lawyers and the proverbial country lawyers. Additionally, these lawyers have succeeded in the thick of things, where competition is often the roughest. This speaks well of their initiative and persistence.

The safest course to follow is to consult initially with a lawyer whose reputation you are familiar with and can trust. This selection should be made irrespective of his office location. If it is difficult for you to travel into the city, you need not think you will be receiving inferior legal services in your neighborhood. The fact is you may get better legal assistance at a cheaper price. It is the lawyer himself and not his office that will ultimately determine whether or not you are satisfied with his work performance. His street address or firm name is seldom material to the judge's decision.

OTHER LEGAL HELP

In criminal cases, you are entitled to a free court-appointed lawyer if you prove to the judge that you do not have sufficient resources to hire your own private attorney. The court will not appoint you a lawyer if indigence is not clearly shown. Even if you are not working, you still may have sufficient assets to disqualify you from having legal counsel appointed.

Many defendants are leary of a court-appointed counsel. They feel such lawyers are controlled by the judge and are not committed to an all-out defense of their case. The reverse is actually true. Public defenders are usually low-paid individuals dedicated to providing full legal services to the poor. They have opted for this type of practice instead of going after far more lucrative positions available to them. They also take far more abuse from judges, who often are annoyed by people defending those who once were deemed automatically guilty but are now receiving fair and sometimes lengthy trials.

Even indigent clients themselves sometime take advantage of the free lawyer. They are more likely to demand a trial, demand motions, and in general be less courteous and candid when they are not paying for any of the time necessarily or unnecessarily exerted on their behalf. The public defender thus "gets it from all sides." In no sense is he "owned" by the court.

Public defenders are employed either by the state, the county, or the city, depending upon the state. Funding is also provided for legal aid offices, which help poor people with legal problems other than criminal law. Legal aid most often represents people in family law and housing law.

Some urban neighborhoods also have nonprofit, community-based law offices staffed by private attorneys. These lawyers are committed to working within a given neighborhood to provide legal services at a reduced rate. They often operate out of a store front or converted home and are generally staffed by younger, dedicated attorneys and local residents.

Many organizations will direct interested people to appropriate legal services. City and state bar associations maintain referral lists of lawyers. In several states, the bar associations lists these lawyers according to their individual areas of expertise. (Bar associations themselves list areas of specialization of their members.) You may call the office of your local bar association if you are in need of a lawyer and don't otherwise know of one.

Private organizations like the American Civil Liberties Union, the National Lawyers Guild, and the National Organization for Women maintain referral lists for specific types of problems; in certain instances, they will take on the case themselves. It is unlikely that the ACLU will write your real-estate trust, but they may be a good starting point if your civil rights have been violated. As a rule, these organizations will take on only those cases whose subject matter is consonant with their philosophy and occasionally their politics. They have all done some extraordinarily important work and are worth consulting where appropriate.

DISSATISFACTION WITH YOUR LAWYER

No one is happy when his case is lost, but in most instances it is only scapegoating to blame the lawyer for the loss. Most lawyers handle their cases to the best of their ability and effort, though when they win the client asserts that he would have won anyway.

It occasionally happens that a client is unhappy with the

performance of his lawyer. This unhappiness may be the legitimate result of a poor piece of work by the lawyer, or the client may feel that the fee charged was simply not reasonably commensurate with the work done.

Most bar associations have discipline boards and fee boards that oversee the activities of their members. In the last few years, these boards have become fairer and more responsive to the complaints of aggrieved clients. It is true that some are rubber stamps for condoning the acts of their brother attorneys. However, the majority of them seem to make an honest attempt to hear all the facts of the controversy and then to resolve it in an equitable manner.

The result for the client may be a dismissal of his complaint, a reduction in his fee, or a censure or, rarely, a disbarment of the offending attorney. It should be recognized that when an attorney is reported for an alleged violation of his fiduciary obligations, his entire lifetime's livelihood is seriously threatened. While you as the client may be very upset, your claim would have to be of an extraordinarily severe nature to terminate a lawyer's career. You must remember that yours was only one case, and all of us are guilty of error. Few of us have our lives ruined because of it. Yet sometimes clients become so angry that they would like to see their lawyer pumping gas for the next thirty years.

If your lawyer has seriously wronged you, you should first try to work it out with him. He should have the opportunity, where possible, to rectify his error or adjust his charges. If after this attempt you are still dissatisfied, then call your state or local bar association and ask for information on the procedures involved with filing for a grievance against an attorney. They will mail you the necessary forms, and you will receive notice of a hearing shortly thereafter.

You also have the right to sue your attorney for malpractice. These suits are extraordinarily costly, time-consuming, and aggravating. They are difficult to prove and difficult to win. As a practical matter, it may be tough to find a lawyer willing to press charges against another lawyer. Just because you lost the case or your lawyer made tactical errors in judgment does not mean he committed malpractice.

Bar associations also maintain fee boards, to consider cases in which only the lawyer's charges are in question. Again, your local bar can provide you with all the necessary information.

HOW DO YOU KNOW FOR SURE?

Of course, there is no sure-fire way to choose a lawyer. Personal prior experience with an attorney or recommendations from others you trust are the most reliable indicators. The other methods of selection described in this chapter vary to some extent in their effectiveness, but each is clearly more reliable than choosing blindly from the telephone book or off the street.

A truly wise person will invest in two or more consultations to get a "feel" for the personality and qualifications of each lawyer as well as ascertaining what each attorney would estimate as an approximate fee. Particularly if you have an important matter in controversy, spending a hundred dollars on two or three initial consultations may prove to be smart shopping that could save inestimable time, money, and worry in the future.

You can be watchful of certain indicators right from your first visit. Does the lawyer seem almost too ready to litigate without first attempting to settle your matter where such a disposition is possible? Is there a time clock on his desk (symbolic or real), and how much does each tick cost? What is his personality? How empathetic does he seem to your problem? What is his experience in the area of your type of problem?

Some considerations are irrelevant. Age, sex, neatness of the office, lavishness of the decor, style of dress, and grayness at the temples are in no sense reliable indicators of the worth of a lawyer. In the end it comes down to the same principles as in anything else: The more careful you are in your selection, the better are the chances that you have chosen a hard-working, honest, and able attorney. Random selections made out of ignorance or prejudice produce sad and often incorrectible results for everyone concerned.

You are paying the money, and the choice is yours.

Index

A

Abatements, 40–41
Abortion, 180
Acceptance of offer, 9–14
Accessory before the fact, 197
Administrators, 98, 108, 116
Advertisements, 11–13, 161–64
Advertising, by lawyers, 238–40
Air travel, chartered, 169
Alcohol, 198
Alterations in will, 101
American Civil Liberties Union, 245
American Psychiatric Association, 192
Annuity, insurance, 86
Appeal of verdict, 233–34
Appliances:
    in apartments, 33, 35
    home, 19–21, 59
Arrest warrant, 207
Arson, 203
Assault, 124–26
Assault and battery, 201
Assignment of a lease, 44
Assumption of the risk, 139
Attempted crime, 196
Automobile:
    consumer complaints, 156–61
    finance of, 156–57
    insurance, 14, 93–95
    purchase by minor, 23

B

Bail, 212–13
"Bait and switch," 162
Battery, 123–24
Beneficiary:
    insurance, 79, 86–87
    named in trust, 113
    named in will, 98
Better Business Bureau, 155, 166
Binder:
    insurance, 83–84, 89
    real estate, 56–58
Bonds, 108–9
Breach of contract, 26–27
Bryant, Anita, 187, 190
Burglary, 204
"Buyer beware," 140–41, 152–53

C

Capacity:
    to contract, 5
    to make will, 100
Capital punishment, 233
"Caveat emptor," 152–53, 170
Charities, immunity of, 150
Chattels, trespass to, 128
Children committing torts, 149–50
Children omitted from will, 110–11
Civil Rights Act of 1964, 180, 182–85
Civil suits, in general, 122
Clamshell Alliance, 187
Class action, 155–56
Closing, real estate, 70–76
Coat checks, 129
Codicils, 103–5
Collision insurance, auto, 93–4
Commission, broker's, 65
Competence of testator, 102
Competitive ratings, 94
Comprehensive insurance, auto, 94
Compulsory insurance, auto, 93
Consent:
    express, 131
    implied, 131
    as privilege, 131–34
Consideration, 6–9, 80
Conspiracy, 196–97
Consumer Product Safety Commission, 161
Contracts, personal service, 16–18
Contract, requirements of, 5–6
Contractual relations, interference with, 148–49
Contributory negligence, 139
Conversion, 128–30
Corporate sale of property, 59
Co-tenants, 42–43
Counter-offers, 14–15
"Covering," 160
Credit, 166–68
Credit cards, 166–68

D

Damages:
    in apartments, 35
    measure of, 26–28
Deceit, 139–42
Defamation, 143–45
Definiteness of offer, 10
Deposit on home, 57–58, 60

Destruction of property, 129
Destruction of subject matter, 18
Devisees, 100
Directed verdict, 230
Disciplinary boards, bar association, 246–47
Disclaimer of liability, 132
Discovery, 217–19
Dividends, mutual companies, 95
Divorce, 237
Divorce, effect on will, 237
Door-to-door sales, 163
Dropping of charges, 215–18
Drugs, 205–6
Drunks, contracts with, 24
Duress, 25

E

Earnest money receipt, 56–58
Eighth Amendment, 233
Employment agencies, 165–66
Endowment policy, 85
Entrapment, 206
Equal Credit Opportunity Act, 168
Equal Employment Opportunities Commission, 182–85
Equal Pay Act of 1963, 181–82
Estimates, 165
Evictions, 47–49, 50
Evidence illegally obtained, 220–25
Executive orders, 184–85
Executors, 97, 106–8, 116
Extended coverage, 92
Extradition, 209

F

Face value, insurance, 84
Fair Packaging and Labeling Act, 160
False imprisonment, 125, 135
False statements, 139–42
Fees, excessive, 244–46
Felonies, generally, 199
Fifth Amendment, 233–34, 229
Fire insurance, 89–92
Forbearance, 8
Force, excessive, 202
Forgery, 203
Forseeability of harm, 137
Fourteenth Amendment, 185–87
Fourth Amendment, 221
Fraudulent contracts, 25
Frustration of purpose, 18–19

G

Gifts, 7
Grand jury:
    generally, 207, 210, 218
    indictments by, 210
    subpoenas by, 210
Guarantees, 19–22

H

Harvard Community Health Plan, 88
Health and accident insurance, 87–89
Hearsay, 228
Holographic will, 100
Home appliances, in purchase of home, 19–21
Homicide, 200–1

I

Illegal contracts, 24
Immigration and Naturalization Service, 191–92
Immunities, 150
Impossibility of performance, 18–19
Indigent counsel, 212, 244–45
Injunction, 148
Injunctive relief, 148
Insane, contracts by, 24
"Insanity" defense, 198
Insects in apartments, 33–34
Insulation, home, 21
Insults, 130
Insurable interest, 80, 88
Insurance:
    automobile, 93–95
    fire, 89–92
    health and accident, 87–89
    home, 65–66
    life, 84–87
Intent, criminal, 198
Intentional torts:
    defined, 122
    generally, 122–30
Interference, with contracts, 148
Interstate rendition, 208–9
Inter-vivos trusts, 113
Intestacy, 98, 100, 115, 117
Intoxication, contracts under, 154

J

Joint enterprise, 196–97
Jury trial, right to, 225–27
Jury venires, 226–27

K

Kaiser Health Plan, 88
Kidnapping, 201

L

Land-sale contract, 58–67
Land, trespass to, 126–28
Lapse of insurance policy, 80–81
Larceny, 203
Lawyers:
    city lawyer vs. local, 242–44
    court-appointed, 244
    disciplining of, 245–47
    fees of, 239
    general practitioners, 236–37
    large firm vs. small, 240–42
    right to, 211–12
    specialists, 237–38
Leases, 35, 38–45
Libel, 143–45
Life insurance, 84–87
List of apartment defects, 35–36, 38
Listings, homes:
    exclusives, 54–55, 56
    open, 55–56

M

Mail orders, 11–12, 162
Manslaughter, 200–1
Marijuana, 206
Marital deduction trusts, 115
Marriage, effect on will, 104
Mason, Perry, 228
Mental distress, 130
Mental incompetents, 154, 198
Minors:
    capacity to contract, 23–34, 154
    committing torts, 136
    criminal acts of, 198–99
Miranda rights, 223–24
Misdemeanors, generally, 199
Misrepresentation:
    of facts, 81–82, 91–92, 155
    tort of, 139–42
Mistrial, 228
Mitchell, John, 187
Mortgages:
    applications for, 68–69
    contingency clause, 61–64
    costs of, 63, 67–68
    interest, 63, 67–68
    processing of, 70–73

Mortgage financing clause, 61–64
Motion to suppress, 220
Moving companies, 169–70
Murder, 200

N

National Lawyer's Guild, 245
National Organization for Women, 245
Negligence, 136–39
Newspaper listings, homes, 54, 56
Nuisance, 145–48
Nuncapative wills, 99

O

Obscenity, judgment of, 205
Offer and acceptance, 9–14
Omitted children's statutes, 110–11
Opinion, 142
Oral promises, 19–22
Oral wills, 99

P

Parents, liability of, 149–50
Parole evidence, 19–22, 58, 60
Partnerships, contracts of, 10
Passing of papers, 70–76
Penalty clauses, 41
Performance of an act, 7
Perjury, 204
Personal service contracts, 16–18
Plea bargaining, 214–15
Pleas at trial, 213–15
Pollution, 146–48
Pre-existing duty, 7–8
Pre-paid health plans, 88
Premiums, insurance, 79–80
Pretermitted heirs, 110–11
Prices, deceptive, 162
Prior course of dealing, 14
Prison system, 232
Privileges:
    consent, 131–34
    defense of others, 134–35
    defense of property, 135
    generally, 130–36, 144–45
    self-defense, 134
Probate of will, 106–8, 116
Probation, 231–32
Promises, 6, 7, 19–22
Promissory estoppel, 28
Property, defense of, 135
Prostitution, 180

Protestors, trespassing, 127
Public defenders, 211, 244
Purchase and sale agreement, 58–67

R

Rape, 201–2
Realtors, 53–57, 65
Receiving stolen property, 203
Rejection of offer, 14
Relief, injunctive, 148
Rendition, 208–9
Rental agents, 31–33, 35
Rent control, 50–51
Rents:
    in general, 31–33
    increases in, 39
    late payment of, 41
    raise of, 45–46
Rent withholding, 49–50
Repair persons, 164–66
Revocation of contract:
    generally, 16–19
    of will, 104–6
Robbery, 201
Roommates, 42–43

S

Schools:
    segregation in, 186
    vocational, 165–66
Search and seizure, 220–22
Sections 1981 and 1983, 188
Security deposits, 36–38
    interest on, 36
    regaining of, 37–38
Self-defense, 134, 202
Sentencing of defendant, 230–34
Shoplifters, 135–36, 208
Sixth Amendment, 226, 227
Slander, 143–45
Sodomy, 144, 190–91, 202
Specific performance, 27
Speedy trial, motion for, 219
Spouse, rights of surviving, 111–12, 116–17
State agencies, 188
Statute of frauds, 22
Statute of limitations, 150
Stolen goods, 128–30
Strict liability, 198
Subleasing, 43–44
Subscriptions, 14
Suspended sentence, 232

T

Tax advantages:
   homeowners, 52–53
   marital deduction, 115
   of will, 98
Tax escalator clauses, 39–41
Tenants, injury to, 138
Tenants-at-will, 45–47
Termination of offer, 14–16
Termination of tenancy, 46–49
Term policy, insurance, 85
Title examination, 70–72
Title VII, 182–85
Torts, parental liability for, 149
Touching, physical, 123–25
Trespass to chattels, 128
Trespass to land, 126–28
Trusts, 112–15
Truth-in-Lending Law, 167–68

U

Unconscienable contract, 154
Undue influence, 102
Unenforceable contracts, 26
Uniform Commercial Code, 15, 160
Unit pricing, 160
"Unnatural and lascivious acts," 202
Utilities, 169

V

Venue, 219
Verdict of jury, 230
Voidable contracts, 22–26, 154–55
Void contracts, 24

W

Warrant, search, 221
Warrant for arrest, 207
Warranty of fitness for a particular purpose, 158–59
Warranty of merchantability, 157–59
Whole life policy, 84
Withdrawal of offer, 15–16
Witnesses to will, 99–100
Written contracts, required, 22